HOW TO REBUILD The BIG-B MOPAR

Arvid Svendsen

S·A DESIGN

CarTech®

CarTech®

CarTech®, Inc.
39966 Grand Avenue
North Branch, MN 55056
Phone: 651-277-1200 or 800-551-4754
Fax: 651-277-1203
www.cartechbooks.com

Edit by Paul Johnson
Layout by Monica Seiberlich

ISBN 978-1-61325-255-0
Item No. SA197P

Library of Congress Cataloging-in-Publication Data

Svendsen, Arvid.
  How to rebuild the big-block mopar / by Arvid Svendsen.
    p. cm.
  Includes bibliographical references.
  ISBN 978-1-934709-37-5
  1. Automobiles–Motors–Modification. 2. Chrysler automobile. I.
Title.

TL210.S956 2012
629.25'04–dc23

2011045065

Printed in China

Title Page:

Once you get the hang of degreeing the cam, it really is a nice insurance policy that the motor is going together correctly.

Back Cover Photos

Top Left:

The camshaft is carefully guided through the cam tunnel so the cam lobes are not nicked or gouged. The cam is also systematically oiled so that it has ample lubrication for first start up and break-in.

Top Right:

Cylinder heads are closely examined before they are sent off to be hot tanked and Magnafluxed or sonically checked. You're looking for cracks, deformations, and other damage.

Middle Left:

In order to get a reasonable look at the condition of the cylinder walls, it makes sense to quickly shoot the walls with some WD-40, and use the stone wheel to remove any built-up corrosion or residue.

Middle Right:

Grinding stones of various angles are used, depending on the desired angle on the seat. For the heads in this rebuild, we are going with a three-angle valve job. The exhaust seats receive three cuts, the top cut (closest to the combustion chamber) receive a 35-degree cut, the seat is cut at 45 degrees, and the bottom cut (closest to the bowl) is radiused, or "rounded out."

Bottom Left:

Although some attach a piston stop across the piston to locate TDC, a dial indicator with a magnetic base installed over piston number-1 accomplishes the same thing with less chance of marking up the piston.

Bottom Right:

With the main bearings installed in the saddles, the main caps with bearing must now be torqued down. Remember, factory bolts require 85 ft-lbs, while the ARP bolts require 100 ft-lbs. Use assembly lube on the bolts in order to produce accurate readings. Torque the bolts in three stages, 30 ft-lbs, 60 ft-lbs, and 100 ft-lbs when installing the ARP fasteners.

CONTENTS

CONTENTS

DEDICATION

To my beautiful wife of 31 years and counting, Gail. She has patiently put up with hours away from the family, as well as days spent in Oklahoma and Arkansas covering the build of the engine. Further, all the hours spent not being "home" while being home, secluded in study for the completion of the writing of this record, were patiently endured by her. While caring for our kids, she tirelessly did all she could to provide writing time for me. Thank you, Gail, for putting up with me during these months of assembling the pages of this book.

ACKNOWLEDGMENTS

There are a lot of great people in the automotive world. I was fortunate enough to have met a number of them in the process of completing the building of the 383 engine for my 1966 Dodge Coronet 500 K/SA car. First and foremost is Jim Lewis, of Jim Lewis Race Engines in Vian, Oklahoma. It is no overstatement to say that Mr. Lewis might be racing's best kept secret. I was fortunate enough to be the recipient of his vast knowledge and experience of building race engines. Always the patient instructor, Jim knows the importance of talking to people. Not simply a spectator, Jim's commitment to building great race engines included racing his bought-new 1969 Road Runner.

Next, I must acknowledge the help and support of my friend and longtime Mopar drag racer Jim Hale. Jim has been drag racing for 55 years, and has long been considered an expert in all things Mopar. When his busy race schedule precluded the building of my engine, it was Jim who steered me to Mr. Lewis. Jim has spent literally hours walking me through the numerous questions of engine theory and history, and I am extremely grateful for his assistance.

My longtime friend and the best mechanic I've ever known, Gene Mosbek, has been instrumental in fueling my passion for NHRA Stock Eliminator racing. Gene has been involved in drag racing for more than 40 years, and is the hardest working drag racer I know. Gene has not only built fast Stockers and Super Stockers, he has also had excellent success as a driver. You always get the straight story from Honest Gene, and his thriving business, Gene's Auto Repair, Elk River, Minnesota, is testimony to his excellent reputation.

Special thanks to Bruce Crandall at Total Engine Service in Bloomington, Minnesota, for coming to my rescue when I needed some technical assistance. Van Senus Machine in Hammond, Indiana, was also helpful in providing photos showing their crankshaft and balancing services. Matt Renz at Midwest Muscle Cars was nice enough to provide space and technical assistance for significant portions of the build. My friend Mark Webster was good enough to lend his expertise in diagnosis and inspection of the engine during disassembly, and I am grateful for his helping hand.

I am not bashful to say that I always sought out what I considered to be the very best parts in the business. I was not interested in second-rate parts for this engine, and I can honestly say that the parts on the 383 are ones that I would use again in an 8,000-rpm rotation of a forged steel crank. In simple alphabetical order, the very best engine components on the planet were supplied by ATI Dampers and Converters, Comp Cams, CP Pistons, Deano's Carburetors, Hooker Headers, Manley Valves, MSD Ignition, RockerArms. com, Smith Machine Lifters, and Total Seal Rings.

WHAT IS A WORKBENCH® BOOK?

This *Workbench*® Series book is the only book of its kind on the market. No other book offers the same combination of detailed hands-on information and revealing color photographs to illustrate engine rebuilding. Rest assured, you have purchased an indispensable companion that will expertly guide you, one step at a time, through each important stage of the rebuilding process. This book is packed with real world techniques and practical tips for expertly performing rebuild procedures, not vague instructions or unnecessary processes. At-home mechanics or enthusiast builders strive for professional results, and the instruction in our *Workbench*® Series books help you realize pro-caliber results. Hundreds of photos guide you through the entire process from start to finish, with informative captions containing comprehensive instructions for every step of the process.

The step-by-step photo procedures also contain many additional photos that show how to install high-performance components, modify stock components for special applications, or even call attention to assembly steps that are critical to proper operation or safety. These are labeled with unique icons. These symbols represent an idea, and photos marked with the icons contain important, specialized information.

Here are some of the icons found in *Workbench*® books:

Important!— Calls special attention to a step or procedure, so that the procedure is correctly performed. This prevents damage to a vehicle, system, or component.

Save Money— Illustrates a method or alternate method of performing a rebuild step that will save money but still give acceptable results.

Torque Fasteners— Illustrates a fastener that must be properly tightened with a torque wrench at this point in the rebuild. The torque specs are usually provided in the step.

Special Tool— Illustrates the use of a special tool that may be required or can make the job easier (caption with photo explains further).

Performance Tip— Indicates a procedure or modification that can improve performance. Step most often applies to high-performance or racing engines.

Critical Inspection— Indicates that a component must be inspected to ensure proper operation of the engine.

Precision Measurement— Illustrates a precision measurement or adjustment that is required at this point in the rebuild.

Professional Mechanic Tip— Illustrates a step in the rebuild that non-professionals may not know. It may illustrate a shortcut, or a trick to improve reliability, prevent component damage, etc.

Documentation Required— Illustrates a point in the rebuild where the reader should write down a particular measurement, size, part number, etc. for later reference or photograph a part, area or system of the vehicle for future reference.

Tech Tip— Tech Tips provide brief coverage of important subject matter that doesn't naturally fall into the text or step-by-step procedures of a chapter. Tech Tips contain valuable hints, important info, or outstanding products that professionals have discovered after years of work. These will add to your understanding of the process, and help you get the most power, economy, and reliability from your engine.

INTRODUCTION

The Chrysler "Wedge" engine family was easily Chrysler's bread and butter from the late 1960s through the early 1970s. Nicknamed for the shape of its combustion chambers, the Wedge demonstrated careful planning and engineering to provide the customer a solid balance of reliability, performance, and utility. Clearly an equal or superior product on the big-block playing field, the Mopar B and RB engines have a strong following among high-performance street car owners. The Wedge stroker engines are strong in stock form and are now available at a very affordable price. Affordable does not mean low quality, as evidenced by a set of stroker rods I recently pulled out of a box that weighed less than 1 gram of one another. Mopar Wedge engines are a logical choice for just about any application, be it street, towing, high-performance street/ strip, or drag racing.

Ask an enthusiast the first word that comes to mind when the subject of Chrysler engines is brought up and it's bound to be the word "Hemi." The Mopar big-block Wedge engine has been forced to live in the shadow of its more famous brother, the 426 Hemi, for decades. How many hopeful eyes have peered into the body-colored engine bay of a Chrysler product, only to turn away in disgust at the absence of the familiar spark plug wires poking through the monstrous valve covers of the iconic street Hemi. Any Mopar aficionado is quick to point out not only the visual impact of the elephant engine, but its rich racing history. Serving as the basic design for engines found in everything from a Top Fuel dragster to a street muscle car, there is perhaps no rival to the Chrysler Hemi in terms of broad range of application.

That said, the Wedge engine is no slouch and is certainly more affordable to build and maintain. Chrysler did not put all its performance eggs in one big Hemi basket. In 1958, the birth of the "B" big-block engine brought 350 ci. From its humble beginnings came a long line of high-performance engines that enjoyed enormous success in a multitude of venues.

Possibly one of the greatest and most popular Mopars of all time, the 1969½ Dodge Super Bee 440 Six-Pack A12 car incorporated state-of-the-art performance pieces to become a legend in Stock and Super Stock racing. Of course, the 440 is a Chrysler RB engine, and the 440 was a staple in the Chrysler line-up from 1966 to 1978. This particular car is owned by Dan Lidberg, and was purchased about 30 years ago for $1,000! Today, the factory two-tone car would be a welcome addition in any collector's garage, especially considering that the unusual color combination and the A12 package makes this Dodge a one-of-one rarity.

Any discussion of these engines begins with understanding that the B series of engines was built with two basic blocks. The B block has been referred to by various names, including "lo block," "low block," and "low deck." This B Wedge engine claimed a deck height of 9.98 inches, accommodating a 3.375-inch stroke. Cubic-inch displacement started at 350, but eventually expanded to include 361-, 383-, and 400-ci versions.

The "RB" block is the second basic block in the B series of engines. It is known by a number of names, including "hi block," "high block," "raised block," and "raised deck." The 10.725-inch raised-deck engine was host to a longer 3.750-inch stroke that spawned the raised-deck 383 in 1959 and 1960, and then the more common 413-, 426-, and 440-ci siblings in what came to be known as the RB engine. The engineering highlights of the new Wedge engine did not go unnoticed.

Rebuild for the Street

Many muscle car guys are content to rebuild their original, numbers-matching engines right back to stock specs. A bone-stock rebuild is logical if the future for their "baby" is a relatively pampered life. But even a bone-stock engine rebuild requires care and attention to proper rebuild techniques and procedures. Building an OEM-spec street engine involves careful selection of components that will make it enjoyable to drive on the street, deliver smooth power, and get very good gas mileage.

Many owners who spend the money for a rebuild want a slight increase in power. For example, an owner often does a performance upgrade in the camshaft depart-

Station wagons are cool. My 1966 Plymouth Belvedere II wagon is an original 361-powered car with factory power brakes and a few other nice options. The car will be used for street duty, and built with a strong emphasis on low-end torque and fuel economy. Do you think a big-block-vintage Mopar can pull 20 mpg or more with the air conditioning running?

ment, supplemented by improved induction and ignition components. Because of the interchangeability in the B/RB engine family, the temptation for building a street engine might be to upgrade the 383-ci engine to a 440. But going from a B-block to the raised-deck RB block means hunting down new brackets for the A/C compressor, so certain factors must be weighed carefully.

The explosion in the automotive aftermarket has made further options for street car owners possible. Over the past 20 years, a number of suppli-ers have developed components that allow you to build an engine with increased displacement by increasing the stroke. Stroker kits can come complete with crankshaft, connecting rods, pistons, pins, locks, piston rings, and main and rod bearings. A stroker kit makes a lot of sense for a street engine, as increased torque and horsepower can be produced while maintaining good street manners. Cylinder heads, camshaft selection, compression ratio, and induction choices must be given careful consideration in order to ensure long-term

This 1966 Dodge Coronet 500 will play host to the 383 engine being built in this book. The car needs some work, but is a good foundation for a Stock Eliminator race car. A Torqueflite transmission will send power to the 5.13 gears in the Dana 60 rear. An ATI torque converter will allow the car to flash to 5,300-rpm launches, while the Cal-Trac bars will help the car launch straight.

reliability and ease of day-to-day usage and drivability. Aftermarket heads available from Edelbrock, Indy, and Mopar Performance can easily be justified in light of power gains and reliability. But then the originality factor goes away, something that is very important to many enthusiasts who are restoring their cars with an eye to returning them to OEM status.

Even a street engine can receive simple upgrades during a rebuild that pays big dividends over time. Though the particular 383-ci B-engine built in this book is destined for the drag strip, most of the same procedures can be employed for building a street engine. The focus is to build this 383 to exacting standards so it performs at its absolute best using many OEM components, while taking advantage of obvious power and efficiency improvements that are available through aftermarket suppliers.

The 440 engine was the center-piece of the most glamorous muscle car offerings in the late 1960s and early 1970s, including the legend-ary 440 Six-Pack, featured in 1969½ A12 cars with a lift-off hood, as well as later muscle car offerings includ-ing 1970 Challengers with shaker hoods. Built correctly, a 440 engine is

Jim Hale NHRA Sportsman Racer

A project of this magnitude could not be handed over to a standard engine rebuilding service. In order for any Stock Eliminator engine to be competitive, an experi-enced Stock Eliminator engine builder and/or racer needs to assemble it. Jim Hale has spent an entire lifetime rac-ing Chrysler products. At the ripe old age of 17, he was already at the drag strip racing his 426 Max Wedge 1957 Plymouth wagon. Jim has owned many Wedge and Hemi-powered race cars. Most recently, his 1967 Barracuda has rocked the F/SA and record G/SA class with effort-less runs well under the class index.

Jim's shop is located in Van Buren, Arkansas, and he is enjoying retirement. He was willing to help with this proj-ect as a final page of his colorful racing career. Consider it a logbook of 50 years in the laboratory of engine research. For decades, his cars have been dominant in class racing.

Known largely for Hemi engines, Jim took a different road in 2003 when he returned to NHRA Stock Eliminator racing. He built a 1967 G/SA 383/280-hp Barracuda. In his own words, "I never raced a 383 until 2005 when I got back into racing. I had sold all the Hemi stuff when I took some time off. When I bought the Six-Pack Challenger formerly owned by Chuck Rayburn, I began to look at the Wedge engines. My Challenger sold quickly to someone who really wanted it, so I studied the books for a new com-bination. I found out that there was a 280-horse engine, rated at 335 horses, in a big car. But that same engine in a Barracuda or Dart was only rated at 280 horses. Nobody ever raced that car with the closed-chamber heads. So I was the first to build a 1967 Barracuda with stock rods

Jim Hale currently races this 1967 383 Barracuda fast-back G/SA Stock Eliminator car that has proven to be a dominant combination. Making the car work with the closed-chamber heads was an accomplishment many other racers had failed to achieve. A frequent top quali-fier, this Barracuda was the motivation for running a similar combination in my 1966 Coronet.

and the 516 closed-chamber heads."

After the success of the 1967 Barracuda stocker, Jim also built and installed a Super Stock 383 engine in this 1968 Hemi SS/AH car, called it a GT/EA car, and subsequently demonstrated another smart move in taking full advantage of NHRA's recent rule changes to allow that combination. In many ways a walking encyclopedia of knowledge, Jim has been instrumental in keeping this rebuild headed in the right direction.

an excellent foundation for a strong performance package.

My 1966 Belvedere II wagon is a typical street-performance rebuild with stock parts. The factory B big-block 361 wagon came with factory air and has been built as a street cruiser. Therefore, the engine going into the wagon focuses on reliability with plenty of torque and drivability for nice around-town grunt.

Rebuild for Stock Eliminator Racing

The underlying axiom of this engine rebuild is that the best way to build a strong street engine is to incorporate race-bred technology and techniques. The goal is to build a big-block engine as close to per-fect as possible, so it is competitive in NHRA Stock Eliminator racing when installed in my 1966 Coronet 500. Because of the rules speci-fied by the NHRA to retain many of the OEM parts when building a "stocker" engine, many of the com-ponents used are the same compo-nents used in a the typical engine rebuild. The 1966 383 engine incor-porates the factory B block, OEM cast-iron "915" small exhaust valve heads, OEM cast-iron intake mani-fold, and numbers-correct Carter carburetor. In other words, even though the engine featured is built to race, I have not forgotten about street engines.

Building a perfect engine used to be called blueprinting. In today's gearhead jargon, people speak more of having an engine "built." I still like the term "blueprinting." It brings back memories of my neighbor's second-generation Corvette. In the late 1960s, he explained to me that his engine had been blueprinted.

NHRA stock eliminator rac-ing demands the very best care and attention so that clearances, toler-ances, and machining are done to the highest possible degree of accu-racy. Time must be taken to make sure that parts are not simply slapped together. Attention to the small-est detail is the order of the day, so that whether your project rebuild is a street engine, bracket racing engine, or even an NHRA/IHRA Stock Elimi-nator Mopar, you gain knowledge to produce the most horsepower pos-sible from largely factory parts.

Jim Lewis Race Engines

Jim Hale steered me to his cylinder head and engine builder, Jim Lewis, of Jim Lewis Race Engines (JRLE) in Vian, Oklahoma. Jim is the original owner of a 1969 383 Road Runner I/SA Stock Eliminator car, and has also raced his orange 1971 'Cuda for years. His prowess with the cylinder heads and overall engine theory com-bined with Jim Hale's aggressive pursuit of power for the 383 combination has resulted in Stock and Super Stock engines that make power.

My first conversation with Jim confirmed his compe-tence. The former mayor of Vian has settled into a brisk and prolific career of building race engines for a number of well-known Stock Eliminator racers. Jim's customers include Tony Hernandez and John Duzac, who are current record holders in Stock Eliminator. But even better than his mechanical experience, is the immediate realization that Jim is one of the good guys. He patiently and thoroughly mapped out a plan of attack for building this engine.

For the record, Jim Lewis is not a Mopar-only engine builder. He has a bunch of Chevy guys out there relying on JLRE power, and his reputation is growing as some-one who makes big horsepower, and charges an honest, fair price for excellent work. As one well-known racer put it, "Jim Lewis might be the best kept secret in Stock Elimi-nator racing." Need an engine built? Take your business to Jim Lewis Race Engines.

Jim Lewis is a well-seasoned drag racer with a number of cars sitting in his engine shop, including this 1971 'Cuda.

PREPARING TO REBUILD THE B AND RB BIG-BLOCK ENGINES

What is it about Mopars? Is it brand loyalty, aesthetics, or genuine superiority of product? If you consider just the muscle car era, say 1960 through 1974, did Chrysler build a better image or a better product? Discussions could go on for hours, but let me say this—the Chrysler big-block B and RB engines bring a lot to the table.

The Family Tree

Before we get started with the rebuild project of my 383 B engine let's look at the introduction timeline of the Wedge series.

1958

By 1958, the new Chrysler engineering department had just been established. After some consideration, Chrysler brass came to the conclusion that the Hemi-head engines were far too expensive and complicated for mass production vehicles and the polyhead design had become somewhat outdated. General Motors had released wedge-chamber-design engines, and Chrysler ultimately did the same with the B- and RB-series engines. The B-series engine was the first new engine platform to come out of the new department. For this model year, Chrysler unveiled its brand-new 350- and 361-ci B-series engine. This new family of engines was quite different from Chrysler's polyhead and Hemi-head engines. The B-series engine featured a wedge-type combustion chamber, hence the "Wedge" nickname.

The new Chrysler wedge engines did not share architecture with the Hemi or the polyhead engines, so parts could not swap between them. The B- and RB-series engines are stout and strong engines. Built as a replacement for the popular Fire-Power engines, the B and RB engines featured meaty cylinder blocks, forged crankshafts, shaft-mounted rocker arms, and wedge-shaped combustion chambers.

Time proved that the new powerplant from Chrysler produced not only strong, reliable power for passenger cars, work trucks, and motor homes, but it was also an excellent foundation for building high-performance street cars and competitive race cars. The B and RB engines became the bread-and-butter engines that propelled Mopars to the forefront of the muscle car golden era from the early 1960s through the early 1970s.

The first B-series engine was the 350-ci. While this was small-block displacement territory, the wedge engine featured big 4.80-inch centerbore spacing, so the cylinders had plenty of room to grow in the future. Many different engines joined the B and RB engine family in the ensuing years. The 350 and the 361 became part of the family in 1958.

1960

The most prolific engine in the family, the 383, arrived in 1960. This engine became a mainstay in Chrysler passenger cars and trucks until 1971.

In 1972, the 400 replaced the 383 assuming its place in the Chrysler lineup and staying in production until 1978. The RB series used the 361 block height and raised it .745 inch. This produced a longer stroke and allowed Chrysler to add more cubic inches to the platform in later years.

The 413 was added to the Chrysler B series family after its initial introduction in 1958. While the standard-fare 413s powered Chrysler Imperials and New Yorkers, a high-performance 413 called the Max Wedge gained fame on the race track. By using a 4-barrel carb, large port heads, an aggressive solid lifter camshaft, and other parts, the Chrysler contingent won countless races at the drag strip.

1963 and 1964

The 426 wedge engine (not to be confused with the 426 Hemi) was a new addition to the RB family in 1963 and lasted only one more year. An evolution of the 413 Max Wedge engine, this Stage II Max Wedge carried many high-performance parts to produce 425 hp. Since this was a race-only engine, you're not likely to find one at your local bone yard.

Another pedestrian 426 was offered in 1964 and 1965, but this was a passenger-car engine that produced 365 hp, and while that's respectable it isn't remarkable. This engine was also offered in Chrysler pickups from 1964 to 1966.

1966–1978

The largest and arguably most notable RB-series engine was the 440, which was introduced in 1966 and continued in production until 1978. This was the largest displacement engine in the Chrysler family for those years. The engine produced exceptional torque and was fitted to a long line of Chrysler intermediate and full-size cars, plus dodge trucks and vans.

Big-Block Wedge Engine Heritage

The following information shows the differences between the low-block and raised-block engines. In terms of usable and reliable performance, racers and street car enthusiasts quickly warmed up to the B and RB Wedge engines. In 1960, the high-block 383, was eliminated and replaced by a low-block 383. The big 4.250 bore and short 3.380 stroke spelled high RPM potential.

B Low-Block Wedge Engines

Engine (ci)	Years	Bore (inches)	Stroke (inches)
350	1958	4.06	3.38
361	1958–1966	4.12	3.38
383	1960–1971	4.25	3.38
400	1972–1978	4.34	3.38

RB Raised-Block Wedge Engines

Engine (ci)	Years	Bore (inches)	Stroke (inches)
383	1958–1960	4.03	3.75
413	1962–1963	4.18	3.75
426	1963–1965	4.25	3.75
440	1966–1978	4.32	3.75

OEM Blocks

Of the two basic blocks, the B wedge engines are the 350-, 361-, 383-, and 400-ci engines, whereas the RB wedge engines are the 1958–1960 383-, 413-, 426-, and 440-ci engines. The B-series engines contain 2.625-inch main bearing journals and the RB engines have 2.750-inch main bearing journals. Both series have extended side walls for increased strength.

Deck height of a B block is 9.980 inches, while the larger RB has a slightly higher deck height of 10.72. Casting numbers located on the sides identify the blocks.

B/RB Cylinder Heads

The B/RB engine is commonly known as a "Wedge" engine because of the wedge-shaped combustion chambers that are strong performers at any stage of tune. From 1958 to 1966, cylinder head design was a mixed bag from street-car design to the all-out, high-performance design of the Max Wedge engines. Though just about any cylinder head can be made to work, the 915 closed-chamber head on the 1967 Mopar big-block engine provided a huge leap in performance. Redesigned ports and larger 2.08-inch intake valves dramatically improved breathing capabilities. Though the standard 915 heads initially dealt with the same smaller 1.60 exhaust valves, the Magnum 440 engine of 1967 introduced larger 1.74 exhaust valves.

As strong as the closed-chamber 915 Magnum heads were, Chrysler produced new offerings in 1968 with new open-chamber 906 heads. The 906 head became common through 1970, and is still coveted as a strong basis for excellent street and race applications. The redesigned 346 casting for 1971 served as the basis for the subsequent 902, 875, and very popular 452 cylinder heads. In fact, racer Herb McCandless said that his OEM cylinder head of choice was the 452 cylinder head, as he saw less cracking in tests.

Block Casting Numbers

These are the most common blocks:

Year	Cubic Inches	B/RB	Casting Number
1959–1960	383	RB	2120 329
1959–1962 Max Perf, truck	413	RB	1852 029
1959–1965	413	RB	2120 529
1959–1965 passenger vehicle	413	RB	2205 697
	413, 426	RB	2468 030
	413	RB	2658 836
	413	RB	2658 930
	426	RB	2659 974
1963–1964 Max Wedge	426	RB	2406 728
(valve clearance machined at top of cylinder bores)			
1964 passenger vehicle	426	RB	2205 697
1963–1965 Wedge & Max Wedge	426	RB	2406 730
1964–1966 Wedge & Max Wedge	426	RB	2432 230
1964–1971	426 Hemi	RB	2468 330
1961–1964	361	B	1737 629
	361	B	2120 229
1958–1966	361	B	2120 329
	361	B	2120 429
1964	361	B	2128 854
1958–1966	361	B	2205 712
1965	361	B	1945 429
1965	361	B	2658 930
1964	383	B	2128 854
1959–1964	383	B	1851 729
1965	383	B	2532 130
	383	B	2468 130
1959–1971	383	B	2568 130
	383	B	2468 403
1970	383	B	2899 830
1966–1972	440	RB	2536 430
1971–1972	400	B	3614 230
1973–1978	400	B	3698 630
	440	RB	3698 828
1973–1978	440	RB	3698 830
1976–1978	400	B	4006 530
1978	440	RB	4006 630

All big-block Mopar cylinder heads were equipped with the rocker-arm shaft assemblies, which were a stronger, more stable design than a typical pedestal design. All B- and RB-series engines built from 1958 to 1962 featured a 1.50:1 rocker ratio. Engines with hydraulic cams used non-adjustable stamped steel rockers. Max Wedge engines came with solid lifter cams and adjustable rocker arms.

Certain Chrysler cars were equipped with better flowing heads, and those included the 300 letter cars and the 440. Differences among these cylinder heads occured in port designs and the open and closed combustion chambers. Open chambers, such as the 906 and later heads, were round and slightly smaller in bore size. Closed-chamber heads, such as the 915 heads, did not have the round combustion chambers that followed the cylinder bore. They instead had a smaller chamber that accommodated the intake and exhaust valves. Most people believed the combustion characteristic of a closed-chamber head was better than the open-chamber design. While the closed-chamber design created higher compression, a flat-top piston design compensated for this in the 383 engine.

Today, heads are relatively available and cheap. All B and RB cylinder heads are interchangeable, but using Stage 1, 2, or 3 Max Wedge heads on a B engine requires a special intake manifold. I purchased two sets of 915 heads for this build, one pair cost $300, the other pair was only $200. It doesn't get much better than that! Obviously, heads should be checked for cracking before purchase, but they can be found.

Cylinder Head Casting Numbers

Year	Cubic Inches	Casting Number	Intake (inches)	Exhaust (inches)
1958–1959	361	1737637	1.94	1.60
1958–1959	361	1944705	1.94	1.60
1960	383	1737637	1.94	1.60
1961–1962	361/383/413	2206324	2.08	1.60
1961–1962	361/383/413	2206924	2.08	1.60
1963	361/383/413/426	2463200	2.08	1.60
1962–1963	413/426 Max Wedge	2402286	2.08	1.88
1964	413 (300K)	2408520	2.08	1.60
1964–1967	361/383/413/426	2406516	2.08	1.60
1964	426 Max Wedge	2406518	2.08	1.88
1963	361-383-413	2463200	2.08	1.60
1963	413 (300J)	2402557	2.08	1.74
1963	426 Max Wedge	2463209	2.08	1.88
1967	383/440	2406158	2.08	1.60
1967	440 Chrysler	2780915	2.08	1.60
1967	440 H.P.	2780915	2.08	1.74
1968	440	2951250	2.08	1.74
1968–1970	383-440	2843906	2.08	1.74
1971–1972	383-400-440	3462346	2.08	1.74
1973	400-440	3462346	2.08	1.74
1973	400-440 "Motor Home"	3751213	2.08	1.74
1974	400/440	3769902	2.08	1.74
1975	400/440	3769975	2.08	1.74
1976–1978	400-440	4006452	2.08	1.74

Crankshaft Casting Numbers

Engine	Application	Type	Casting Number
413	Truck 8–bolt crank	Forged	1521 436
350	1958 car	Forged	1737 642
361	1958–1961 car	Forged	
383	1959–1961 car	Forged	
413	1959–1964 car	Forged	1851 127
413	1960–1977 truck 8–bolt crank	Forged	1851 436
383	1959–1961 car	Forged	1855 527
RB	1959–1961 car	Forged	1978 698
B	1959–1961 car	Forged	2203 155
361	1960–1978 truck 8–bolt crank	Forged	2206 157
440	1966–1972 car, 1971–1977 truck	Forged	2206 158
413	1962–1965 car	Forged	
426	1963–1965 car	Forged	
400	1971–1972 car, 1972 truck	Forged	
383	1962–1971 car, 1967–1971 truck	Forged	2206 159
361	1962–1966 car, 1972–1978 truck	Forged	
440	1966–1978 car, 1970–1980 truck	Forged	
413	1962–1965 car	Forged	2206 160
426	1963–1966 car	Forged	
426	1963–1964 Max Wedge	Forged	2402 330
426	1964 Max Wedge, 8–bolt crank	Forged	2463 548
383	1971 2-bbl	Cast	3462 923
400	1971–1978 car, 1973–1979 truck	Cast	
400	1973–1978 car, 1973–1979 truck	Cast	3751 877
440	1973–1978 car	Cast	3751 888
400	1973–1978 car	Cast	4027 172
440	1973–1978 car, 1973–1979 truck	Cast	4027 175

Crankshafts

Crankshafts in Wedge engines are a bit complicated. One of the benefits of the B and RB engines is that they all came with forged-steel crankshafts until 1971, and these are very strong and resilient crankshafts. These cranks are certainly adequate for most high-performance applications, but it is wise to groove main bearings for adequate oil supply at higher RPM. Back in the day, raised-block-engine owners were able find a 413/426 Ramcharger Super Stock crankshaft (PN 2406240). This forged-steel crank was flame hardened and much stronger than the stock unit. Today these rare crankshafts are expensive collector items that are difficult to find.

The cast crank was introduced in 1971 in the 383 engine with 2-barrel carb, and later showed up in the 2- and 4-barrel 400-ci engines. The cast cranks have a six-bolt flange and use specially balanced vibration dampeners and torque converters. Engine builder Jim Lewis typically limits the usage of the cast crank to the lower horsepower, stock rebuild engine.

The B low-block and RB raised-block engines have different strokes and different main journal diameters. The low-block engine has a 2.625-inch main journal diameter, while the RB engine has a 2.750-inch main journal diameter. Those differences call for different-size bearings and also mean that B- and RB-series crankshafts do not interchange. Make sure to check bearing sizes before installation.

413 and 426 Max Wedge

By 1962, the 383 was available in a Plymouth or Dodge with two

4-barrel carburetors, pumping out an advertised 343 hp. But the real news in 1962 was the brand-new Max Wedge 413 engines. These engines grew to 426 ci with a 4.25 x 3.75 bore and stroke and were offered through 1964, lasting through 1965.

The change from the 413 to the 426 saw performance improvements, and the 426 engine was offered in two versions: a 415-hp engine with 11.0:1 compression and a 425-hp engine with 13.5:1 compression. The 1963 and 1964 Max Wedge B-Body cars, such as the Dodge 330 and 440 and the Plymouth Savoy and Belvederes, enjoyed great success at the drag strip and have shown themselves to be the most highly sought after Mopars among diehard Chrysler fans.

Years went by with the 383 low-deck engine serving as the Chrysler entry-level powerplant. But the raised-deck RB 440 that first showed up in 1966 in the big C-Body cars was soon installed in the lighter B-Body cars, such as the 1967 Plymouth GTX and Dodge Coronet R/Ts.

Intake Manifolds

Most Chrysler B and RB engines were equipped with cast-iron intake manifolds and topped with Carter AFB 4-barrel carburetors. The main exceptions were the Max Wedge race engines that used a cross-ram intake rather than a conventional design. From 1967-on, the 440s were equipped with a higher-flowing manifold design than the earlier ones. In addition, the 383 fitted to larger B-Body muscle cars also used the higher flowing manifold. The 440 was equipped with three 2-barrel Holleys, dubbed the Six-Pack, and if your engine is equipped with this intake, you should retain it. Edelbrock made the manifold for 1969 engines while Chrysler made it for the 1970 model.

Exhaust Manifolds

Like a majority of the other OEMs, Chrysler used cast-iron exhaust manifolds but the port size and runner length varied according to the model it was fitted to. The 1967–1971 440 manifolds flow better than other B and RB cast-iron exhaust manifolds. The Tri-Y manifolds for the 1964 426 Max Wedge are very rare.

Building a Street Engine

I have two projects that fuel the flame for building Wedge engines: one is a street car, and the other will be an NHRA Stock Eliminator car. My street car is based on a classic American station wagon built by Plymouth in 1966. This particular Plymouth Belvedere II station wagon came with the B 361 big-block engine, factory air conditioning, power brakes, and steering. The wagon will be receiving a Wedge engine that will produce somewhere in the neighborhood of 350 to 400 hp, be rock solid in the reliability department, and get decent gas mileage for extended use, like Power Tour or overnight muscle car events. Cruise nights, local car shows, and family outings call for a nice lopey

If this engine looks a lot like your engine, you've come to the right place. The 361 will be removed to make way for a rebuilt 383 street engine. It needs to be reliable, produce decent power, and get good gas mileage. Fully loaded with air and some options, the wagon weighs about 4,000 pounds, so it needs to produce a healthy amount of torque. Pulling a big-block Mopar from any 1962 to 1970 B-Body Chrysler requires similar methods and tools.

*Big-block Mopars were built from 1958 to 1978, and showed up in just about any car or truck line that Chrys-*ler offered during that run. For that reason, finding a core engine is still relatively simple. The 383-ci 4-barrel engine had been removed from a 1966 Chrysler, and was complete from carb to pan. I bought the engine for $250, which is about right for a 383 core. Expect to pay closer to $400 for a complete car or truck 440 engine. Of course, any high-performance version will be higher.

idle, and 3.23:1 gears makes the car livable on the highway.

A stroker engine is a very good possibility if you are looking for a great performing engine with excellent street manners for cars, custom trucks, and street rods. Stroker kits can be sourced from just about any of the major performance houses, such as Speed-O-Motive and Mopar Pro Shop. Many builders believe the ultimate stroker engine is a 451-ci version, created by placing a modified 440 crankshaft into a 400 B block.

There are a number of reasons that a 451-ci-stroker engine is popular. The shorter deck height means a lighter block, the lower deck height and longer rod and stroke of the 440 rods and crank allow for a lighter piston, and all the accessories of a car originally equipped with a B engine, like my wagon, bolt on. Andy Finkbeiner's *How to Build Max-Performance Mopar Big-Blocks* is the definitive source for more information on stroker combinations and possibilities based on both the B and RB big-block Mopars.

High-Performance Engine Rebuilding

The express purpose of this book is to show you how to rebuild a Mopar B or RB big-block engine so it provides strong reliable service, like the day the engine was fired up for the first time. But I am taking the rebuild process a step further than a garden-variety stock rebuild. I am rebuilding a 383 low-deck B engine using OEM factory components for the purpose of NHRA Stock Eliminator racing. My intent is to focus on the blueprinting of this engine. The major tenet is to incorporate many of the techniques used in this race engine into your street or race engine. Ultimately, the challenge for you is to get your car out of the garage and drive it.

Building a Stock Eliminator engine has evolved over the past 50 years, but there is still enough of the soul of the sport left to make it highly appealing. This engine will have a factory block, rods, crank, heads, intake, and carburetor. NHRA Stock Eliminator racing allows aftermarket rods, pistons, and camshaft and valvetrain components, but many of those items would likely be considered for a mild street build. Given the time and resources, it's safe to say that any owner is committed to having his car running as strong as possible. Stockers live by that creed.

Stock Eliminator racing is a performance class, built around the challenge of getting the optimum performance from factory pieces. For that reason, the diligent rebuilder will be able to take the necessary steps to build a perfect engine. Clearances, tolerances, settings, and adjustments are carefully optimized. When the engine is complete, it will be run on the dyno, and tuned for maximum horsepower. It will then be raced on a limited basis in some NHRA divisional events, as well as some local bracket meets.

Engine Build Philosophy

A few factors go into building a strong "torquer" engine. One of the key, even critical, factors to building torque is creating optimum cylinder pressure. An engine that is able to efficiently take in a denser air/fuel mixture, by definition, creates more heat during combustion, thus higher cylinder pressure that turns the crankshaft with greater force. This simple principle lies behind supercharging, which operates on the benefit of cramming the densest air/fuel mixture possible into the cylinders.

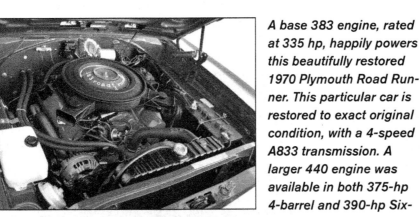

A base 383 engine, rated at 335 hp, happily powers this beautifully restored 1970 Plymouth Road Runner. This particular car is restored to exact original condition, with a 4-speed A833 transmission. A larger 440 engine was available in both 375-hp 4-barrel and 390-hp Six-Pack versions, as well as the optional 426 Hemi engine. The 383 was also an excellent performer in the big B-Body platform.

The 1962 Plymouth 383 with factory dual-quad engine has been a popular combination over the years, and Jerry Bennet's outstanding D/SA post car is one of the best ever built.

Cylinder pressure depends on the combination of the piston, ring package, final honing, and camshaft selection. The combination of our 383 Stock Eliminator engine calls for CP forged pistons, Total Seal gapless rings, Comp Cams Stocker Cam, and Jim Lewis' 30 years of expertise in final honing.

Another key factor in building torque is airflow velocity. Certain applications that are not limited in intake and exhaust port size might not have to worry as much about airflow velocity as does the stocker application that requires the use of factory heads, factory carb, and factory intake. If the air/fuel mixture cannot depend on port volume, it must instead employ high velocity to fill the combustion chamber. Though piston ring seal again plays into the velocity of the airflow, an unimpeded path created by proper valve and valve seat preparation is essential.

The third key factor in building torque has to do with camshaft selection. Recalling that Stock Eliminator can only work with stock lift, the valve must stay open long enough to achieve optimal volumetric efficiency for filling the combustion chamber. Intake lift for the 383 is .425 inch, and not much better is the .437 lift on the exhaust. Fortunately, the 2.08 intake valves and 1.60 exhaust valves are not too bad.

NHRA has recently changed the rules from allowing a three-angle valve job, to a multi-angle valve

For NHRA Stock Eliminator drag racing you can only run a 9-inch racing slick, but recent development has proven that the skinnier tire is capable of running cars deep into the 9-second ETs. The leaf-spring unibody platforms of the 1960s and 1970s Chryslers are excellent platforms for quarter-mile competition. With simple modifications, the drivetrain can be made close to bulletproof. Bottom line? A Wedge-powered Chrysler product has proven itself to be one of the greatest grass-roots drag cars of all time.

High-Performance with Reliability

Although racers often talk about "making power," the truth of the matter is that the focus should be on making torque. In Jim Lewis' words, "Torque gets the car going, horsepower keeps it going." Though Stock Eliminator racing is essentially bracket racing during eliminations, the thrill of the occasional head-to-head race and winning class when the event has class scheduled makes the class much more than a bracket race. If the car doesn't "60 foot" well, there is little hope in winning a head-to-head race. So, the focus has to be on torque.

Of course, much more needs to be said about building torque, but the focus from Jim Lewis Race Engines is cylinder pressure, airflow velocity, proper camshaft selection, and perfecting the valvetrain for reliable and effective breathing.

Most of the techniques and information concerning the build of this 383 apply to both B and RB engines. However, the short stroke of the B engines have an impact on how this engine is built versus a stroker engine. Much can be accomplished using OEM parts.

job. Lewis and his flow bench have become very good friends over the years, and each valve is carefully optimized for flow on the backside of the valve and the flow at the valve seat.

The performance pedigree of the B/RB big-block Mopar engines is rich. The performance potential of the Wedge is continually developing as it receives up-to-the-minute aftermarket attention.

Choosing the Right Race Car

There are at least a few principles that influence your choice of car to race. The first principle is to love the car you race. It doesn't matter whether other people love your race car, build it for you. My race car project is a 1966 Coronet 500, easily one of my top two favorite muscle cars ever built. It might not be yours, but it is mine! Bottom line? Interest quickly fades if the car that is being raced is not something that produces pride of ownership. Though any muscle car is quick to produce excitement, I would have to concede a strong passion for any B-Body Mopars from 1962 to 1970.

The second principle is to build a car to be competitive. Surprisingly, this Coronet should be very competitive in Stock. The landscape today includes a number of brand-new 2008 through 2012 Ford Mustang and Dodge Challengers built from the factory that are tearing up NHRA Stock Eliminator. Until the cars are factored properly, the thinking is usually to either buy one of the new factory cars or race in a lower class so as to avoid a head-to-head run with them. Though my Coronet can fit as high as I/SA, options exist to run the car in H or J, depending on total weight of the car at race time.

The third principle for building a stock eliminator race car is to build something you can afford. My Coronet can be built for about $30,000, using an engine builder, chassis guy, and painter. However, if you have a lot of parts laying around and can do much of the work yourself, that cost can be less.

A horsepower-to-weight ratio system determines the classes for NHRA Stock Eliminator. NHRA begins with factory horsepower ratings, and adjusts those ratings depending on performance of the combination, sometimes by the requests of racers, or by outrageously fast performance at the track. Changing the NHRA horsepower rating is not easy, and adjustments are typically in small increments. NHRA wants to see a particular combination tested and flogged before it is willing to refactor an engine.

If an engine is shown in the real world of drag racing to be severely underrated from the factory, NHRA adds horsepower to the rating. Conversely, if it can be demonstrated that the factory rating is high, NHRA might be more likely to subtract horsepower to make a combination competitive. Honestly, there are very few sleeper combinations that have been overlooked; most world beaters have already been discovered.

Gene Mosbek races this factory lightweight 1964 Plymouth 426 Max Wedge Savoy in A/SA Stock Eliminator. "Stockers" are popular because they are strongly linked to the 1964–1972 golden era of muscle cars, they present the challenge of building the fastest car under strict rules, and they are awesome to watch. Stock and Super Stock racing experienced a surge of popularity with the arrival of the new-generation, factory-built Challenger Drag Pak, Mustang Cobra Jet, and Chevrolet COPO Camaros.

My 1966 Coronet is fairly competitive on paper. The 383 engine was rated from the factory at 325 hp in 1963. However, NHRA rates this engine at 280 hp. That rating is more in line with reality, and makes it a wise choice for someone wanting to participate in an entry-level type of drag racing. Cam lift is decent, the carburetor is adequate, and the 915 casting heads permitted by NHRA for the 1966 383 are pretty good for building horsepower. The Coronet should be able to run high 11-second times, placing it in the middle of qualifying right out of the box.

TOOLS AND CLEANING EQUIPMENT

In order to complete an engine rebuild, a fairly extensive collection of tools is necessary. Various stages of the project call for equipment that might not be found in an average tool box. For that reason, factor in the cost of renting or purchasing tools and equipment that is necessary to rebuild the engine. The money saved by doing the work on your own typically covers the cost of the tools, but again, budget and plan.

Though much of the focus on engine building centers around parts and machining processes, keeping everything clean is an absolute necessity for building a strong, reliable engine.

Basic Hand Tools

A full line of hand tools is necessary for rebuilding an engine. My favorite brand is Craftsman, though a number of other suppliers are available and acceptable. No tool chest is complete without a set of 1/2- and 3/8-inch-drive ratchets, six- and twelve-point sockets, spark plug sockets, and various length extensions. Preparedness also calls for a full assortment of open- and box-end wrenches, screwdrivers, pliers, wire cutters, Vise-Grips, Allen wrenches, scrapers, knives, various levels, a tap-and-die set, pry bars, and hammers.

High-end consumer tools with a lifetime warranty provide excellent performance and reliability. Avoid inexpensive, off-brand tools without a warranty. These tools are often rough cast and are not precision made, making you much more likely to round off bolt heads, break fasteners, and strip screw heads. As a result, you save a little money on tools but give yourself a lot of headaches. If you've ever had to tap a bolt because you broke off a

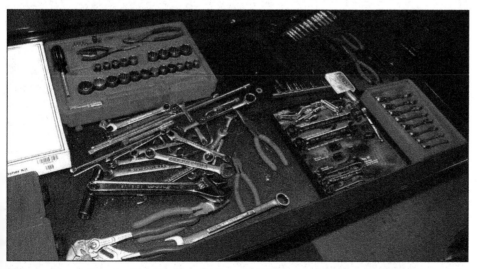

You need a full assortment of basic hand tools to complete any engine rebuild. Always use high-quality tools, such as Craftsman, Husky, or similar brands with a lifetime warranty. If you can afford professional tools, such as Snap-On, Mac, or others, go ahead and buy them. With these tools, the quality of your work should be exceptional.

bolt head, you know that it's tedious and time-consuming work.

In addition, if your B or RB engine hasn't been rebuilt recently, engine parts are often rusted together from exposure to the elements, oil, carbon, and heat cycling. That means disassembly is often challenging.

You need to the follow the proper procedures, select the right chemicals, and of course, use high-quality tools.

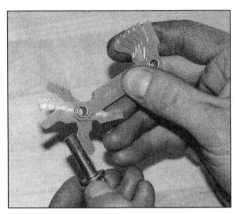

It's a good idea to have a thread gauge on hand to guarantee that the proper bolts are installed in the engine. Simply hold the gauge to the bolt, and determine if the bolt is the consistent thread needed for the application.

Once the engine has been prepared for removal, rent or buy an engine hoist. Affectionately referred to as a cherry picker, the best option may be to rent one and avoid the high cost of buying it. Further, storing one of these beasts after purchase is often a problem.

Working at Jim Hale's shop allowed us the use of a hydraulic lift, which made engine removal simpler and easier. Even if the car is on jackstands, a floor transmission jack is the smart way to install a transmission. Essentially, a hydraulic jack with an adjustable plate to hold the transmission, the transmission jack makes removal and installation a walk in the park.

New or used, an engine stand is a must-have for rebuilding your big-block Mopar that tips the scales at about 620 pounds. Engine stands have various weight ratings, typically 750 or 1,000 pounds. Some are rated for 1,500 pounds; safety easily warrants the extra expense.

Here's a homemade trick from Jim Hale: after removing the transmission, the engine is virtually suspended on the engine pads without the added support of the transmission mount. This simple bar with a couple home-bent J-brackets rests on the torsion bars to support the engine. The support bar is placed on the torsion bars, and slid under the back part of the oil pan for an extra measure of support and safety.

One of the crucial instruments needed in rebuilding an engine is a dial bore gauge. This one made by Mitsutoyo is accurate to .0001 inch. Expect to spend close to a thousand dollars for a comparable unit. Here it is being used to check the main bore, something that is done while installing the main caps to ensure proper machining. The dial bore gauge allows checking for accuracy along the entire bore, and indicates if any final honing is needed.

A torque wrench allows you to tighten the bolts to spec as listed by the manufacturer. By doing so, the engine components properly seat to their respective mating surfaces. Shown is a click-type torque wrench (which sells for about $80). The older beam-style torque wrench measures torque on the fastener with a pointer, but is less accurate. A high-quality torque wrench starts at about $200. For most home engine builders, a Craftsman or Rigid click-type torque wrench is adequate. If you intend to splurge on a few expensive tools, one of them should be a high-quality torque wrench.

Required Specialty Tools

Specialty tools are often very expensive, so weigh the cost of purchasing them with the amount of time you will use them. If you're simply rebuilding a single engine, renting these tools from an auto parts store or using a friend's specialty tools is the way to go. If you're rebuilding several engines, these tools quickly pay for themselves.

A good dial indicator is invaluable in checking clearances for deck height, valve reliefs in the pistons, and a number of critical measurements. Dial indicators often have a magnetic base to simplify mounting.

Here are a variety of micrometers for taking critical component measurements while assembling the engine. The open mouth allows for measurement of pistons, bearings, and other critical components.

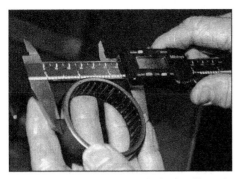

Mitsutoyo's electronic digital caliper is one of the best on the market. Claiming accuracy to +/- .0005 inch, the digital readout is more precise than a dial caliper, and far easier to use. Less expensive versions are available from Craftsman, Snap-on, and Matco.

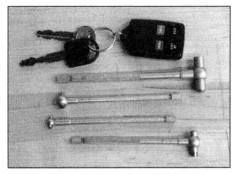

A telescoping snap gauge can be used to accurately measure various-size holes, such as lifter bores. By centering the telescoping piston in the bore to be measured, a micrometer determines the amount of the piston's travel created by the size of the hole.

A valve height tool measures the installed height of the valve, necessary for dialing in proper valvetrain geometry.

When ring gaps are right, the rings are installed on the piston, and a piston ring compressor compresses them so that the piston can be inserted into the block. For setting the proper ring gap, the ring is placed in the cylinder, squared with a ring squaring tool to ensure that the ring is square to the cylinder wall, and then the gap is measured.

The amount of time spent preparing cylinder heads for reinstallation requires a set of cylinder head stands. Designed to sit on a workbench, these stands avoid the constant moving and repositioning of the head that is necessary when rebuilding it.

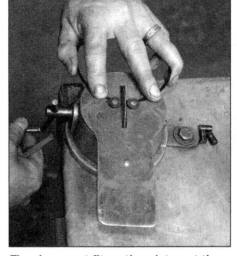

The ring must fit on the piston at the precise specification supplied by the manufacturer. To attain that spec, rings must be filed to the proper amount and checked again.

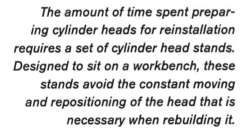

Though a stock rebuild does not necessitate degreeing in the cam, any serious engine rebuilder takes the time to make sure the cam and entire valvetrain is optimized for cylinder pressure and power. This Pro Degree Wheel by Mr. Gasket is perfect for the job, but there are a number of other companies that offer a degree wheel, including Comp Cams. Using a dial indicator with a magnetic base and a rigid pointer, degreeing in a cam is essential to ensure that the camshaft is phased correctly with the crankshaft. A newer digital tool for degreeing a cam is also available for those who prefer the high-tech approach. The digital tool has an advantage in being able to work in a smaller space, such as when the engine is already installed.

HOW TO REBUILD THE BIG-BLOCK MOPAR

Spectre offers this engine lift plate, which gives you the ability to create a lift point for engine removal. The lift plate bolts to the intake manifold using the carburetor mounting holes. The engine hoist simply hooks up to the holes on the vertical plate.

Cleaning Equipment

Although the initial disassembly and engine cleanup removes years of built-up grime, parts washing and scrubbing is a continual task during block prep, balancing, component fitting, and final assembly. Even the smallest shaving can cause cylinder scoring, bearing failure, or connecting rod breakage. Patience and perseverance in thorough cleaning habits pay big dividends for the investment being poured into your engine rebuild. In fact, the choice of a machine shop might stand or fall based on its commitment to cleanliness.

The factory dampener on my 383 that was disassembled did not need a puller-type dampener removal kit. Many dampeners, however, need to be convinced to be relieved of duty. A simple dampener removal kit makes life easy, as the three-prong arrangement attaches to the dampener while a center-drive bolt drives the dampener off the engine.

Proper engine cleaning calls for a full program of equipment, tools, and supplies. A splash of cleaner on a newly balanced rod is not the practice of a first-class machine shop. Look for the professionals to spend pend time scrubbing, brushing, and continually inspecting for the proper removal of grease, dirt, and metal shavings. Debris can adversely impact engine operation and bring about false torque readings during assembly. Something as simple as an improperly cleaned thread impacts future serviceability and repair.

An amazing technological advance for the professional engine builder, a profilometer is able to measure proper cylinder hone roughness. Essentially, this tool takes the guesswork out of determining the finish hone on the cylinder walls. Expect to pay about $3,000 for one. For the professional who makes his living making horsepower, this tool can greatly increase the quality of the finish of a customer's cylinder walls.

As Jim Lewis explained, "I build all my motors the same, what one guy gets, the next guy gets. And the motors are built the way I would want an engine built for myself."

A good valvespring compressor is necessary for cylinder head assembly. Manual versions are an option. However, if you plan on doing any extensive head work, experimenting with different valves and cuts, and anticipate constant maintenance on your valvetrain, then a pneumatic valvespring compressor (shown) is the way to go. Of course, an adequate air compressor is necessary as well, with air lines and fittings.

In addition to washing parts and keeping them clean, the block and cylinder heads need to be cleaned with various shapes and sizes of brushes. Goodson offers an excellent engine brush kit that meets the needs of block prep and cleaning. A complete Mr. Gasket Engine Cleaning Brush Kit (PN 5192) is available for about $40, which includes a nice assortment of brushes needed for the job.

ENGINE REMOVAL AND DISASSEMBLY

Before tearing down your engine, you need to do a few helpful and necessary things. If your engine is not damaged and still runs, doing a simple compression test on the engine helps diagnose the condition of the engine. Low compression in a particular cylinder should be noted and examined more closely during teardown. Low compression can be the result of a number of problems, including worn head gasket, worn rings, or poor valves or seats. If you are working on a tight budget, a compression test is especially helpful in determining which parts need replacement and which parts can be used in the rebuild.

The key to this important step is careful organization and storage of the removed parts. Have Baggies, boxes, labels, ties, and Sharpies ready to meticulously label all parts and wires. If that buddy helping you wants to get this engine out and apart in an hour, send him home. Keeping track of where parts go and how they came from the factory makes assembly more organized, less time consuming, and far more enjoyable.

The focus of this rebuild is a 1966-vintage 383 engine that I purchased from Craigslist.org for $250. The seller told me, "I had it running . . . it ran rough, but it ran," but disassembly proved otherwise. My newly acquired 383 had the main components needed for a rebuild, but it had not been running for years and was essentially frozen. A frozen engine is not necessarily the end of the road for your donor builder core, but it is not the ideal.

Find an engine that spins freely, and verify the fact that it spins over.

If you have access to an actual shop with a hydraulic lift, you are able to quickly and safely remove the engine from your vehicle. I elected to remove the transmission and the engine separately, so being able to work from underneath the car on the lift made things much easier.

Fortunately, upon disassembly, my $250 builder core cleaned up nicely with a .060-inch overbore.

Hood Removal

Find a partner to help remove the hood from the car. Before loosening the hood hinge bolts, disconnect the wire to the underhood light, if so equipped. There's nothing worse than trying to do that while holding the hood with both hands. Each person must have a 9/16-inch ratchet. Loosen the two bolts per side using one hand to hold the hood. As the bolts loosen, the hood slides down and can easily damage the cowl area, so hold the hood firm. Once the bolts have been removed, lift the hood and set it aside.

Tear Down

Disconnecting the battery is the very first step in the tear-down process. Make sure you are wearing safety goggles and some type of mechanic's gloves. Though some may scoff at the idea of wearing proper safety glasses, the simple process of disconnecting a battery brings potential risk.

Remove the negative cable with a 7/16- or 1/2-inch open-end wrench. An adjustable crescent wrench also does the job. The negative cable is typically black. When the negative cable is disconnected, remove the positive cable, usually red in color. If the positive side is removed first, you could potentially damage the electrical system of your vehicle by simply brushing it against other metal.

I strongly suggest removing the battery from the car completely so as to avoid having something drop on it, or getting bumped as the engine is being removed.

Cleaning Supplies

To make the process go smoothly and more efficiently, buy all your engine cleaning supplies before you start. To prevent rust, don't stop until all the engine parts are treated. Be sure to get five gallons of solvent, powdered laundry soap, a 5-gallon bucket, some rolls of shop towels, white lint-free shop rags, an engine cleaning brush kit, and a rust inhibitor, such as WD-40.

Original Status Documentation

One of the realities of the automotive hobby is the tragedy of unfinished projects. Far too many well-meaning enthusiasts dig into a project without documenting the original condition of their engine bay. You need to start from the beginning, which means taking pictures of every conceivable angle of the engine, every fastener, every line, and every component that is found in the engine compartment.

If a camera is not available, take extensive notes and make drawings and diagrams, which enable you to return all lines and fittings back to their original location.

Jackstands

After taking detailed pictures, it is time to get the car positioned for engine removal. If you are working in your garage, park the car so you can crawl underneath it from either side. Using a hydraulic floor jack, lift each side, and place a jackstand underneath the rear frame rails.

Never go under a car that is supported only by a floor jack. Use a broom or something similar to move the jackstands into position. I like putting the jackstand just behind the front of the spring perch where the frame rail is still flat. Do not have the jackstands too high; only high enough to get the tires off the ground.

Go to the front of the car and place the jackstands under the K-member, and lift the front end of the car on each side. Again, place jackstands at the lowest settings underneath the front frame rails on both sides of the car. Slowly lower the car until all the weight of the front of the car is resting evenly on all four jackstands. At this point, stand to the side of the car and push the car sideways with increasing strength to make sure it is resting securely and safely on those four jackstands.

Drain all fluids before removing the engine by opening the petcock along the bottom of the radiator. Make sure you catch the coolant in a large enough drain pan because there can potentially be close to 2 gallons of coolant in a running vehicle. Drain the engine oil by removing the oil drain plug and allowing the oil to drain into a proper oil drain pan. Dispose of all fluids properly.

If there is any unsteadiness or shifting at all, start over and find better resting points for the car on the jackstands. Better that you find out now that the car is not positioned securely on the jackstands, rather than when you are underneath it.

Never use cinder blocks to support a car—they are not strong enough to handle the weight. They can easily break after having been wrongfully used to support a car, so again, only use good-quality jackstands that can be trusted to support the vehicle.

Transmission Fluid

If your car has an automatic transmission, drain the transmission fluid. Unless you have a transmission pan with a drain bolt, drop the transmission pan in order to drain the fluid. Use a large enough drain pan so that the transmission pan can be placed in it upon removal.

Make sure no linkage or cooler lines interfere with removal of the pan. If there is interference, those items need to be removed.

Begin to remove the bolts that hold the transmission pan in place. As you loosen the bolts, transmission fluid begins to drain out the sides of the pan. Without proceeding any further, and with the pan somewhat still in place, allow the transmission fluid to drain as much as possible. Continue to loosen the pan, stopping to allow fluid to continue draining. Eventually, the pan can be removed and placed in the drainage pan.

Air Conditioning

If the car is not going to undergo an entire restoration, do not remove the A/C lines from the compressor to the firewall. Instead, unbolt the A/C compressor from the engine, lay it to the side against the inner fender panel, and use wire or twine to position it out of the way during removal. If you decide to leave all the A/C lines intact, you should be able to remove the engine without harming the A/C compressor.

Radiator and Fan Shroud

The radiator, fan, and fan shroud must be removed. Place a large drain pan underneath the radiator, and unscrew the petcock at the bottom of the radiator to allow the coolant to drain. Many petcocks become frozen over time. If such is the case with your vehicle, drain the coolant by removing hoses very slowly. Remove the lower radiator hose after the coolant has been drained from the radiator via the petcock. Make sure you position a large pan on the floor to catch the escaping coolant. Then remove the upper radiator hose, both heater hoses, and any hose running from the water pump.

If you choose to remove the heater hoses at the firewall where they connect to the heater core, do not twist the hoses, as that will likely damage the heater core. Instead, take a razor blade and slice the hose until it is free from the heater-core connection.

Most of the coolant should be drained at this point, but there is still a significant amount of coolant in the engine itself, which might spill out as you begin pulling the engine from the engine bay.

There are two bolts along each side of the fan shroud to remove. Once the fan shroud is free, move it back over the engine fan. If you have an automatic transmission, remove the transmission cooler lines from both the radiator and the transmission. The lines might need to be nudged so they can be removed, but they should eventually come out. Do your best to save the lines by not forcing them out, as they can be reused after a simple cleaning. If you kink any part of the line, replace it when reinstalling the engine.

The 1966 Belvedere II wagon had been purchased partially disassembled. All front radiator and heater hoses had been removed, as well as the front accessories. If your car still has the hoses in place, take time to remove them using either a screwdriver or an adjustable wrench.

If your hoses are cracked and rotted, you can simply cut them off using a utility knife. If they are in good shape, use a pick or cotton pin puller to work under the edge of the hose and pull it off its fitting. At the same time, use an adjustable wrench to disconnect the transmission lines that are connected to the radiator. You do not need to remove the alternator and power steering pump at this time, as it is much easier to do so with the engine sitting on a stand.

Once all lines and hoses have been removed from the radiator, lift it straight up and out of the engine compartment, being careful not to damage the fins, which are both sharp and easily bent. Once the radiator is removed, lift the fan shroud away from the fan and out of the engine compartment. Four small bolts retain the fan itself, so remove the bolts and remove the fan from the engine.

Fuel Line, Belts and Electrical Wiring

All fuel lines and electrical lines need to be removed. Make sure to label all lines with masking tape and a Sharpie. When you remove the fuel line at the fuel pump and at the carburetor, place a rag under the fuel line or a small plastic cup to catch any leaking fuel. The fuel line spring clamps can be stiff and fairly difficult to reach.

The alternator and power steering belts could become a nuisance if left on the engine during removal, so loosen the attaching bolts on both the alternator and the power steering pump, then remove the belts. Make sure to mark the belts before setting them aside.

Throttle and Shifter Linkage

Extreme care must be taken to not bend any rods or brackets when removing throttle and shifter linkage. A bracket mounted to the engine secures the throttle linkage. Mark the location where the cable is attached to the bracket to ease adjustment at the time of reinstalling the engine.

Whenever possible, return nuts and clips to their proper location after being removed. Be extremely careful with small clips and fasteners that could be difficult to locate.

Take plenty of pictures to document location of the fasteners and any special steps in the disassembly process. Place all linkage parts in Baggies, with clear labels and instructions for re-assembly, as if someone else will be putting the car back together in the future.

Distributor

It is not necessary to remove the distributor and wires in order to accomplish engine removal, but doing so prevents the distributor from being damaged. If you choose to do so, remove the spark plug wires and factory wire separators and hold-downs. Many times the hold-downs only need to be cleaned before being transplanted to the new engine to help make the new engine installation look factory correct.

Organization During Disassembly

A successful rebuild requires slow and painstaking attention to every detail of the disassembly process, including every part removed from the engine. It is highly unlikely that even the best mechanical minds are able to remember and recall every single clip, clamp, bolt, bracket, and component that comes off a Chrysler big-block. My personal theory is that many parts are sold on eBay and at swap meets because the originals were misplaced during a rebuild through lack of organization. What should have become a freshly rebuilt, like-new engine for a very fun car actually became a disorganized pile of junk, with unknown parts and pieces that have little value.

Carefully make a list of everything you need to properly label, collect, itemize, and store the parts you remove. On your list should be plastic bags that close and come with labels (buy an assortment of sizes) and a five-pack of Sharpies. Also get masking tape, labels, tags, smaller boxes of various sizes, plastic grocery bags, and whatever else you think of.

Make sure to have a place where all parts can be stored together, protected from contamination and damage. For example, do not store an extremely valuable date-correct carburetor separately from all other items out of fear of losing it. Sometimes putting a part in a very safe place is tantamount to losing it. Have a couple buckets and large plastic containers available as well.

In order to mount the engine to an engine stand, bolt the stand's rear plate to the engine. Hoist the engine carefully and insert the plate's head into the stand. Be sure the engine is balanced on the stand, and have someone assist you in moving it. If the engine seems unbalanced, reposition the stand head to the engine. Make sure to fully tighten the bolts.

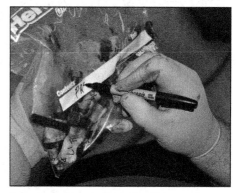

Label and bag all parts. Have a few boxes or containers ready for some of the bigger parts, such as the power steering pump and the alternator. Keeping the bags of fasteners and brackets with their corresponding component makes reassembly much more efficient.

While the 361-ci engine was pulled from the wagon, we are rebuilding a 383. Externally, the 361 and 383 are virtually identical. This particular engine is a 1964 383 2-barrel engine with air conditioning out of a Dodge 440. I'm leaving the A/C compressor and power steering pump on the engine during cleaning, but I have removed the alternator. You might have to remove the flexplate or flywheel from the engine prior to attaching the engine stand head.

Remove Components

1 Remove Universal Joint

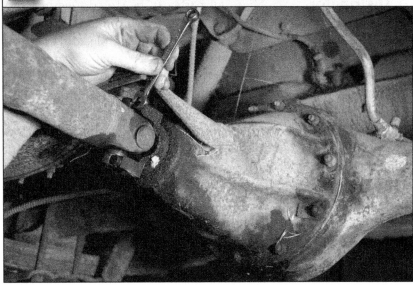

In order to remove the driveshaft you must first remove the rear universal joint. A 7/16-inch open-end wrench handles the job nicely. The wagon came with an 8¾-inch rear differential, which is likely strong enough for most street/ strip applications.

2 Remove Exhaust System

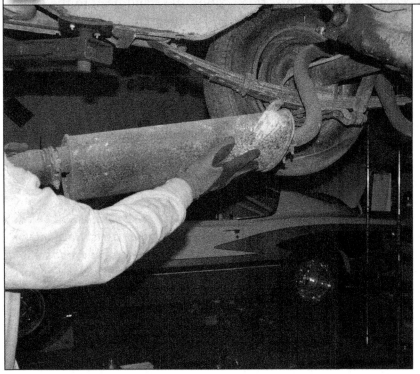

In the case of the wagon, the exhaust system was removed and trashed. The exhaust manifolds on the 361 were in good shape, and only needed to be unbolted to remove the front portion of the exhaust. If the exhaust manifold fasteners on your engine are frozen, soak them with your preferred penetrant, and let the manifold sit for a few hours, and repeat if necessary. If the bolts are still frozen, apply heat from a propane torch, but avoid getting the bolts red hot. If the bolts break in the head, you either need to remove them later, or have a machinist do it.

3 Remove Battery Ground

Unbolt, label, and set aside the battery ground. Disconnect, label, and lay aside all other wires and miscellaneous parts in preparation for engine removal. Take your time, an hour saved by rushing through tear down will likely bring a tenfold share of problems during assembly.

4 Remove Flexplate Dust Cover

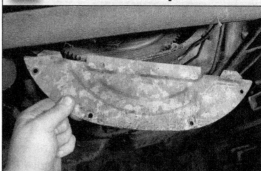

Remove the flexplate dust cover to gain access to the torque converter bolts. Four bolts hold the dust cover in place. Using a 7/16-inch wrench or socket, remove the four bolts, and the dust cover can be removed. You are then able to see the flexplate that attaches to the converter/starter ring gear assembly.

5 Detach Flexplate

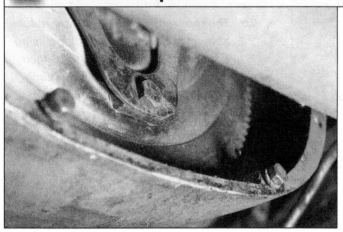

Since room is limited, you need a 1/2-inch open-end wrench, preferably with a long handle, to remove the four bolts that attach the OEM flexplate to the converter/starter gear assembly. Use a large breaker bar on the center crankshaft pulley bolt to lock the engine while removing the bolts. Because these bolts are somewhat protected, they come out quite easily. Spin the engine with the breaker bar to get the flexplate to turn so you can gain access to the other bolts.

6 Rotate Crankshaft

Place a long-handle box-end 1¼-inch wrench on the balancer's center bolt to turn over the engine to gain access to each of the four flexplate bolts. Once the bolts have been removed, remove the transmission. If the engine is seized, you cannot gain access to all four flexplate bolts. In that event, you have to remove the engine and transmission as a unit from the vehicle.

7 Unplug Front Wiring Harness

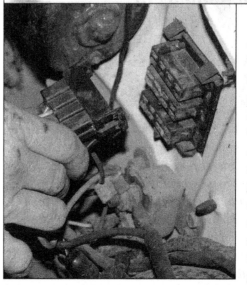

The front wiring harness unplugs at the firewall. This removal might be the first time the plug has been moved in more than 40 years, so avoid being impatient, or you may harm either the wires or the plug itself.

8 | Remove Transmission Lines

Locate the transmission lines, and place a drain pan underneath them on the floor. Using an open-end 5/8-inch wrench, disconnect and, if possible, remove the transmission lines that run to the radiator. Depending on the type of vehicle, it might be easier to manipulate the lines without actually removing them, saving actual removal of the lines until after the transmission and/or engine is out of the car. Regardless of the condition of the lines, set them aside and do not throw them away (you should keep them for reference if you buy or make new transmission lines). You also need to remove the shifter linkage and the speedometer cable that attaches to the transmission. Be careful to tag and bag all shifter linkage parts, as there are a number of clips and fasteners that are incorporated in the linkage. The tendency is to start ripping through parts, and not organize all the little pieces. Resist this temptation and do not say to yourself, "I'll just buy new parts." Even if you are absolutely convinced that this car is getting that Turbo Action shifter, do not throw these parts away.

9 | Remove Top Transmission Bolts

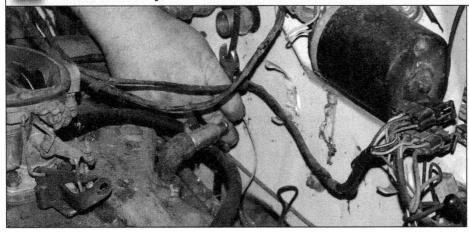

The top transmission bolts are reachable from the top of the engine using a long-handle, open-end, 9/16-inch wrench. The angle needed to reach the bolt can lead to stripping the bolt if you are not careful, so take your time to make sure the wrench makes complete contact with the bolt head.

Special Tool

10 | Attach Engine Lift Stabilizer Bars

Lift the homemade Hale engine support bar into place. The brackets rest on the torsion bars, while the bar is snugged up against the bottom of the engine. The major purpose of the bar is to avoid the scenario of the entire weight of the engine resting on the engine mounts with no rear support that would normally exist via its attachment to the transmission. Taking the time to fabricate this handy little item makes you feel a lot better about the engine hanging in the engine compartment while not attached to the transmission.

11 | Remove Remaining Bolts and Crossmember

After soaking in WD-40, the remaining transmission bolts come off quickly and easily. Again, use the long-handle, open-end, 9/16-inch wrench to help you reach the remaining bolts. Next, remove the transmission crossmember bolts that attach to the body. Leave the center portion of the transmission crossmember on the transmission. Doing so avoids the potential of denting the transmission pan when setting it on the ground or a dolly.

12 Pull Transmission

Be sure the car is in the optimum position for transmission removal. Place a transmission jack under the transmission pan (a rag or towel helps keep the transmission from sliding around as it is lowered). Carefully move the transmission rearward to detach it from the engine. If you don't have the luxury of a lift, and are working on the floor under the car, make sure you have placed the car on four jackstands with enough room for the transmission to be removed from beneath the car. (As a safety precaution, create a backup in case the jackstands fail. For example, a properly positioned railroad tie under the front K-frame could save your life if the jackstands fail.) Use a transmission jack to lower the transmission from the car, while making sure you have someone with you under the car to keep the transmission from dropping to the ground.

13 Remove Engine from Engine Bay

Using a 5/8-inch socket or wrench, loosen the engine-mount bolts, but do not remove them. From underneath the car, we were able to get at the bolts with a cordless drill with 5/8-inch socket attachment, but you might have to use a different approach, depending on how your car is positioned.

Attach winch cables or a chain to opposite corners of the engine. Use a couple of large washers and bolts that match the thread of the intake manifold bolts and are about 2 inches longer to make room for the cable ends. Make sure the wiring harness has been disconnected from the engine, and that all wires and lines are no longer attached to the engine.

Use a winch or hoist to lift the engine slightly to take some weight off the engine mounts. Remove the engine-mount bolts using the 5/8-inch wrench or socket wrench. Slowly lift the engine out of the engine bay. If you are using a standard cherry picker, lifting the engine requires some arm pumping action and does not allow you to use both hands for steadying the engine as it is lifted out. Make sure the engine remains stable. If it begins to swing, you might damage the firewall, brake booster, or radiator support. This engine was removed in about an hour. Without a vehicle lift, figure two to three hours to remove a transmission and engine.

13 Remove Engine CONTINUED

The electric winch in the shop that removed the 361 engine suspends the engine until it is attached to a portable engine hoist. You might want to bolt it up to an engine stand.

14 Remove Alternator

For less weight on the engine stand, and in preparation for cleaning, remove the alternator. The alternator is attached with 9/16-inch bolts, but it makes sense to have open-end/box-end wrenches and sockets for the 3/8-inch-drive ratchet in sizes 7/16, 1/2, 9/16, and 5/8 inch sitting in a cart near the engine so that any replacement or oddball bolt can be removed. A pneumatic gun makes the process faster. Have a few screwdrivers, scrapers, and a medium-size Vise Grip on hand for the disassembly process. Save the brackets for future use, though other possibilities exist for relocating the alternator.

15 Bag All Parts

Label and bag all parts. Have a few boxes or containers ready for some of the bigger parts, such as the power steering pump and the alternator. Keeping the bags of fasteners and brackets with their corresponding component makes reassembly much more efficient.

16 Clean Engine for Disassembly

It is time for the engine to be scrubbed externally. If you have access to a portable engine hoist, this is the better way to go for cleaning. Rather than having the engine on a stand with the chance of tipping while it is being scrubbed, the hoist seems safer. Additionally, the grease and grime running off the engine does not have to run down the stand or collect in the stand. Use a high-quality engine degreaser to strip the engine of grease, grime, and oil. For this rebuild, I used Gunk Foamy Engine Cleaner and Engine Degreaser. Both products are effective for cleaning the exterior of the engine, but the Engine Degreaser is more aggressive than the Foamy Cleaner.

Mix about 1 cup of concentrated soap with 1 gallon of water. Scour the block using the soapy solution and brushes or lather up the block and then rinse it with a pressure washer. Vigorous brushing improves cleaning. On this particular engine, though it looked fairly clean, a lot of grime had built up over the years.

Be sure to wear gloves and eye protection during this cleaning procedure. Spray the engine degreaser on the engine, being especially generous on the areas where grease and grime have accumulated. Follow the instructions on the can as to how long the chemical sits on the grease before rinsing. After scrubbing, thoroughly rinse the engine. If you have access to a pressure washer, use it, being careful to not damage any fragile parts that might still remain on the engine. If Gunk Foamy Engine Cleaner does not strip off the heavier areas of grime that were still on the engine you can try Easy Off oven cleaner.

Engine Disassembly

1 Drain Oil Pan

If the oil was not drained at removal, remove the drain plug and drain the oil pan. Also remove the oil filter and lay it in the drain pan. Make sure to put the drain plug back in the pan when the oil has drained out completely.

2 Remove Ignition Coil

The ignition coil attaches via a clamp-style bracket that bolts to the intake manifold. One of the bolts of that bracket is shared by the A/C compressor bracket. Use a 3/8-inch-drive ratchet with an extension and a 9/16 socket to remove the two fasteners that mount the ignition coil.

3 Remove Air Conditioning (If Equipped)

In the 1960s, automotive air-conditioning systems were gaining in popularity, but still somewhat primitive in design. For that reason, don't be surprised as to how big and bulky the A/C compressor is.

It is attached to the engine with a series of stout brackets. Remove all fasteners on those brackets, but be sure to take several pictures of how this attaches to the engine. (If you have the space during storage, leaving the brackets attached to the compressor greatly reduces a mountain of frustration trying to figure out which bracket goes to which hole.) The A/C compressor uses two support brackets that attach to the intake manifold, and a mounting plate to the engine block.

To remove the engine, the A/C compressor must be laid aside from the engine. Some cases require that the compressor be removed completely. Look at the mounting configuration of the A/C compressor and soak all bolts with penetrant. The bolt at the base of the driver-side support bracket requires a 5/8-inch ratchet. The passenger-side support bracket that runs to the intake manifold requires a 9/16-inch ratchet for removal of the bolt that attaches to the intake manifold.

Remove both bolts, and then examine the bracket holding the ignition coil. Your compressor is likely mounted there, as well. You have to remove that attachment, and it requires a 9/16-inch wrench. Reach behind the compressor and remove the bolts to the mounting plate. If you have hard lines that run from the compressor to the condenser, remove them. In order to do so, you likely have to evacuate the system to comply with state and federal regulations (check your local laws).

If your lines are flexible, you can lay the compressor aside, and wire it away from the engine. Mark the bolts with the nuts and washers, and keep them with other parts related to the A/C. After all fasteners have been removed, and all the brackets are free and clear, remove the A/C compressor, which weighs about 25 pounds.

4 Remove Ignition Coil

With the coil freed from the intake manifold, use a smaller crescent wrench to carefully remove the two nuts and washers that hold the contact wires to the posts on the coil. Then put the nuts and washers back on the posts of the coil so it can be used again.

5 Remove Distributor

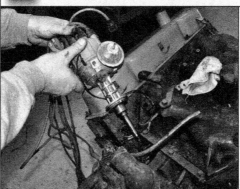

Use a 1/2-inch open-end wrench to loosen the bolt on the distributor hold-down located where the distributor shaft enters the block. Lift off the distributor clamp and tag it for reassembly. Once the distributor clamp has been removed, lift out the distributor and store it in a safe place. Keep the wires on the cap, and mark each one as to which cylinder it fires. I simply use masking tape on each wire, and mark each masking tape with a black Sharpie. By doing so, you save yourself about 15 minutes of frustration trying to figure out which wire stretches to which cylinder. You are also less likely to confuse the firing order during installation.

6 Keep Track of Parts

Remove and label the idler pulley and all attachment brackets. If you lose these, you won't find them at the local boneyard, so keep track of all of the accessory brackets and fasteners! Losing or misplacing rare, hard-to-find parts can result in a massive parts hunt that can take months or longer. Disassembly is all about organizing and taking careful inventory of everything that comes off the engine.

7 Remove Power Steering Pump

Use a 9/16 wrench to remove the power steering pump. Since there is still fluid in the power steering pump, keep one of your hands on the outlet hole. Remove the three bolts that mount the pump. When the pump is removed, check it for leaks, a free-spinning pulley, and overall condition. (Do not throw these items away, as they could be original with date stampings and codes that could fetch big money at swap meets or online auctions.) If you keep the pump from tipping over, you can drain the fluid after it is removed. Again, make sure to save and catalog all the brackets, spacers, and fasteners that hold your particular power steering pump in place.

8 Remove Water Pump

You can remove the water pump if you prefer, but I chose to leave the entire water pump housing together. Using a 9/16-inch socket wrench and open-end wrench, remove the water pump housing fasteners. If you soak the fasteners with penetrating spray, they unthread without great difficulty. Often the water pump housing stays stubbornly attached to the engine, so use a block of wood as a base for the pry bar to gently work it loose. Do not gouge the metal during this process. By patiently tapping at the housing, it should work loose. Resist the temptation to bludgeon it because you may end up breaking or scarring it.

9 Unbolt Exhaust Manifolds

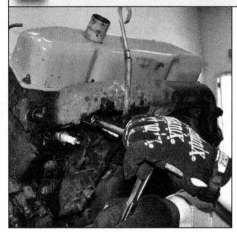

Use a 9/16-inch wrench and 1/2-inch ratchet wrench with extension to remove the exhaust manifolds. Prior to attempting to remove the nuts, soak the bolts with WD-40 or similar penetrant. Progressively apply pressure to the wrench to remove the bolts. If they do not come off immediately, a breaker bar might be effective, but you risk breaking the bolt and thus complicating removal.

If you are not able to remove a bolt, again soak it with a WD-40–type product, and let it sit for a few hours. If that does not work, you can use a small torch to put some heat on the bolt to break it loose. The heat causes the metal to expand enough to possibly break it loose from the threads. After heating the bolt, get a good hold of it with a pair of Vise Grips.

A last-resort method for removing a frozen bolt is to grind the head off, and then drill out the shaft of the bolt using a small, hardened bit.

10 Remove Valve Covers

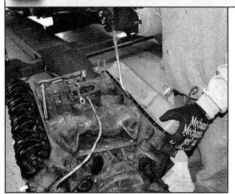

Fortunately, these valves covers were properly installed and barely needed a touch from the pry bar. If your valve covers are cemented to the block, wrap the pry bar with a plastic sleeve or some masking tape to avoid gouges and kinks in the metal. Seeing all the rockers and pushrods in place is an indicator that your engine has not experienced valvetrain failure.

11 Unbolt Fuel Pump

Remove the mechanical OEM fuel pump, which should always be replaced or rebuilt. Make sure you have a catch pan under the fuel pump as it is being removed, because it is likely that some oil will leak out as it is being removed. Watch also for any lingering fuel in the pump or fuel lines. In the case of this engine, which had been in hibernation, only a shellac-like residue remained from the fuel.

12 Remove Front Accessory Pulleys

The upper and lower front pulleys must be removed. The upper pulley is attached with four fasteners, while the lower crank pulley has six fasteners. You need a ratchet wrench and a 1/2-inch socket with an extension to reach into the pulley. The center bolt that attaches the harmonic balancer does not need to be removed in order to remove the pulleys.

If the pulleys turn, get a partner to help keep the engine from turning with a wood wedge against the back of the pulley. (On this particular engine, once the attachment bolts were removed, both upper and lower pulleys literally dropped off.) If the pulleys do not come off easily, spray penetrant around the fastener holes and the center of the pulleys, and attempt to spin or wiggle them until they break free. Do not hit any of the pulleys for removal, as they are prone to bending.

Mark the pulleys, fasteners, and center bolt, and even create a diagram of how they install. Inspect all the pulleys for unusual signs of wear, cracks, and damage. If you hear or feel binding when you spin the pulleys, you have to replace the bearing.

13 Remove Carburetor and Intake Manifold

Take detailed photos of the fuel lines, vacuum hoses, throttle cable position, and all other notable details. Then unbolt the carburetor from the intake manifold. The intake manifold must be removed using a 9/16-inch socket. Prior to removal, liberally douse the fasteners with penetrating spray. As the engine comes apart, hidden areas open up, sometimes revealing debris. Clean up each area before going any further.

Even with all fasteners removed, don't expect the intake manifold to lift right off the engine. You may have to pry the intake manifold off, so be sure to pry between the intake and head surfaces with something that does not gouge or damage them.

Under the intake manifold is a thin aluminum valley cover, so if a gentle tap from a soft-faced hammer does not do the job, get that wooden wedge and lift up on the manifold from the block itself. Because the manifold is heavy and at an awkward angle, find a second person to help you lift the manifold off the engine to prevent any injury.

14 Remove Intake Valley Pan

Once the intake manifold is off, remove the valley pan. It is held in place with two retaining plates, which use three 7/16-inch fasteners per side. Use a ratchet wrench with an extension and a 7/16-inch socket to remove the fasteners. Use a scraper to break the valley pan free from the head intake port surfaces. Since this part must be replaced, do not worry about bending it. This pan keeps the oil away from the intake manifold, which lowers the temperature of the intake manifold, making for a cooler intake charge.

15 Replace Valley Pan

The valley pan is inexpensive and should be replaced for the rebuild. Otherwise, you risk an improper seal and leakage. This one was well used and will be replaced.

Documentation Required

16 Remove Rocker Assembly Shaft

First, remove the valve covers. Use a socket and ratchet to remove the retaining bolts. Use a 9/16-inch socket to remove the rocker arm shaft assembly. Remove the bolts and retainers and carefully label and store them.

Here is one of the reasons why the Mopar big-block Wedge engine is such a good candidate for performance builds: the rocker arm shaft assembly. The rockers mount and pivot on the shaft, making it more stable at higher RPM. To make it even more reliable for drag racing, our rocker arm shaft assembly will be rebuilt by rockerarms.com (formerly Rocker Arm Specialist).

Valvetrain Organizer

Summit Racing offers this Comp Cams valvetrain organizer. The tray is labeled front and rear and allows you to organize all the valvetrain components in the installed order from the engine. Each lifter, push rod, and rocker must return to its original position because these valvetrain assemblies develop unique wear patterns, and the components should not be mixed up and used on other cylinders. Buy this tray even if you are replacing the entire valvetrain because it helps in diagnosing the condition of the engine, or any cause of an engine problem or failure. (The center holes are used for spark plugs.)

Documentation Required

17 Label Rocker Arm Shafts

When you remove the rocker arm shaft assembly fasteners be very careful to label them because they are different lengths. A diagram can be helpful in identifying where the longer and shorter fasteners attach. Include one in the Baggie that contains these fasteners.

18 Place Rocker Assembly on Valvetrain Organizer

Lift off the entire rocker arm assembly and lay it on the valvetrain tray.

Professional Mechanic Tip PRO TIP

19 Remove Push Rods

To remove the pushrods, lift them straight out after the rockers have been removed. A quick test to see if a pushrod is straight is to roll it on a straight and level surface, such as a piece of flat glass or straight table surface. Rolling it slowly, make sure you see no daylight between the table and the pushrod. Place the push rods in the correct position on the valvetrain organizer.

20 Remove Hydraulic Lifters

Pour some 30W oil on the lifters to aid removal. A hook tool may be needed to pull some of them out. Some are even more stubborn, and must be persuaded with a gentle tap from a hammer and a punch. If you must go this route, be extremely careful to avoid damaging the lifter bore. If some lifters won't come out at all (as was the case in our disassembly), wait until the rest of the bottom end of the engine has been disassembled. With the entire bottom end of the engine open, you should have room to position one hand under the lifter while pushing on the top of the lifter with the other hand.

21 Remove Cylinder Head Bolts

Spray penetrating lube on the head bolts prior to removal, and let it soak in. Prior to removing the head, simply loosen two opposite-side outside bolts and pry off the head with a wooden handle. The object is to break the seal from the head gasket. The heads are located on dowel pins, so if you lift the head enough, it breaks free even from the dowel pins. Be careful, as the cast-iron heads weigh about 45 to 50 pounds. You do not want to drop them and possibly injure yourself.

When the heads move just slightly, stop prying, and see if the heads are still partially sealed to the block. If further prying on the head is necessary, do so. If it is completely freed, place the head back in the installed position where it is located by the dowel pins. Put the wooden handle aside, and remove the remaining bolts. Do not worry about the heads dropping off, because the dowel pins hold them. Determine where you are going to set the head, and carefully lift the head off the block and set it down.

22 Remove Crank Dampener

Loosen the OEM-style center bolt with a 1¼-inch socket employing an air gun or breaker bar. With the center bolt removed, use a puller similar to one seen here to remove the OEM dampener. (The puller can be rented from parts houses and some local auto parts stores.) Do not attempt to pry the dampener away from the engine. Use a 1/2–inch ratchet wrench to attach the puller to the dampener with the supplied mounting bolts and be sure the bolts extend by 1/2-inch into the dampener.

Lubricate the puller threads with engine oil or spray lubricant. Using a 1/2-inch socket on a 3/8-inch-drive ratchet or breaker bar, thread the puller until it snugs down on the crankshaft and then continue to turn the puller as it pulls the dampener off the crank snout.

Important!

23 Remove Timing Cover

Remove the timing cover using a 1/2-inch deep-well socket. VERY IMPORTANT: Two bolts are common to the oil pan and the timing cover. In other words, you must remove the two oil pan bolts that join the timing cover in order to remove the cover. If the timing cover doesn't come off, it is likely fused onto the engine through heat cycling and grease. As those two bolts come off, make sure they don't fall into the catch pan.

24 Remove Timing Chain and Gear Set

Use a socket and breaker bar or a wrench to remove the OEM-style center bolt. The timing chain and gear set should easily lift off the crank and camshaft, but if installed for years, these parts may not lift directly off. There is a strong probability that it needs some persuasion from a soft-faced hammer. Carefully tap the gear and wiggle it until it comes loose.

25 Remove Distributor Drive

Remove the distributor drive gear before carefully lifting the camshaft out of the cam tunnel. This gear needs to be closely inspected, as it drives a new MSD distributor. Your initial observation may be good, but it likely needs to be replaced.

26 Remove Camshaft

Using a 5/8-inch socket, loosen the camshaft bolt. With the cam bolt, attach the cam handle to the front of the cam. If you do not have a camshaft handle tool, consider purchasing one because it makes camshaft removal and installation much easier and allows you to guide the cam through the tunnel to help prevent damaging it. You can remove the cam old-school by grabbing the cam and working it out. The cam is difficult to handle, so be careful as you guide it out, so as not to damage the camshaft. Again, some 30-weight oil can help this process, but take your time because you don't want to damage the cam lobes or the cam tunnel.

27 Remove Oil Pump

With the cylinder heads off, the external oil pump must be removed. Three bolts hold the pump in place. Use either a 9/16-inch wrench or ratchet to remove the pump. The pump should simply lift out of the block. Oil is the lifeblood of the engine and you don't want to risk a new engine on an old pump, so make the wise move and buy a new oil pump.

28 Remove Oil Pan

After draining the oil, reinstall the drain plug. Within a few days, oil will again accumulate in the pan. Rather than spinning the engine over allowing all that residual oil in the pan to run through your engine, remove the pan Once the pan has been removed, rotate the engine so the crankshaft is at the top.

29 Remove Oil Pump Pickup and Tube

The oil pickup and tube comes out next. The pickup tube is threaded, so use two hands to turn it counterclockwise and it should come off. If it does not move, don't force it. You could easily kink the pickup tube, and not be able to reuse it after a thorough cleaning. Grab a pair of locking pliers, and cover the jaws with plastic sleeves that can be purchased at a parts store to keep the tube from being marred. If you do not have plastic sleeves, wrap the jaws with masking tape. With one hand on the pickup and pliers at the base of the tube, it should turn.

Critical Inspection

30 Remove Main Bearing Caps

Visually inspect the two-bolt main caps to see if they are in good shape. To be safe, they should be Magnafluxed to confirm that they are usable. Main journal number-3 is the thrust bearing. To measure crankshaft endplay, loosen the thrust bearing with a 3/4-inch socket.

31 Remove Main Cap Number-3

Main cap number-3 is the thrust bearing, so it is removed to examine for wear and any damage. Hence, there should be no unusual grooves, marring, or other damage. Reinstall the thrust journal. Seeing that our rods were stamped and numbered, and one of the rods had been balanced, it's a good guess that this engine had previously spun a bearing, and all the bearings were then replaced.

32 Measure Crankshaft Endplay
CONTINUED

This dial indicator reads .007 inch, which is within spec. So far so good, therefore the engine seems to be a good candidate for a rebuild, but it needs more scrutiny before making the final decision.

34 Separate Connecting Rod Caps

My engine was seized, so turning the crank to access the rod bolts was not possible. If you are able to turn the crank, you can access the rod bolts with ease. Remove each rod cap separately by using a 1/2-inch-drive ratchet or breaker bar with a 9/16-inch socket to remove the connecting rod bolts. Loosen the bolts on the connecting rod and apply a few firm taps with a soft-faced hammer to separate the connecting rod halves. Use the soft-faced hammer to drive the nuts downward and separate the connecting rod cap from the crank journal. Once that is done, remove the cap and bearing. Tag them and set them aside for eventual assembly. Use a number stamp on the rods to identify the cylinder number.

32 Measure Crankshaft Endplay

Mount a magnetic base or clamped base to the block so the dial indicator can be positioned properly. Place the dial indicator on the front snout of the crank to measure crank endplay, which should be no greater than .007 to .010 inch. Any more than that indicates excessive wear and abuse. Use a large pry bar to push the crank forward and back.

33 Remove Pistons

It is conceivable that the pistons could be used again, so prior to removing them, number each one to keep them organized.

Upon removal, store all the pistons, connecting rods, and bearings in the order they were removed from the block.

35 Inspect Connecting Rod Cap

Oil underneath the rod caps is a good sign. These bearings have been replaced at some point in the past. Look at the rod caps themselves for any unusual signs of wear such as grooves or scratches. In most cases, it's a wise choice to replace well-used stock connecting rods because these parts are under enormous stresses and they do lose their strength over time. In many cases, a typical connecting rod with more than 100,000 miles on it has reached the end of its service life. For any rebuild with more than 400 hp, use a high-quality I- or H-beam rod from a reputable manufacturer. At this point, there is little reason to conclude that this engine is not an excellent choice for a rebuild.

36 Remove Pistons From Cylinder Bores

Line up the rod with the cylinder and place a wooden dowel or the wooden handle of a hammer under the dome of the piston. Use a plastic mallet to tap the piston-and-rod assembly out of the bore. Be sure to catch the piston and rod as it emerges from the bore because you don't want it to hit the floor. A block reamer is only necessary if you remove the piston out the top of the engine, which is not a recommended method. A ridge reamer is a crude tool that can easily damage a block. Therefore sending the pistons out the bottom of the engine is the preferred method. Have the machinist remove the ridge at the top of the cylinder walls created by excessive wear or poor lubrication.

To remove the connecting rod caps, use a piece of hard wood to tap the piston out of the hole. If you have a couple pistons that are frozen in the block, do not despair. The block may still be a good foundation for the rebuild project. To remove the frozen pistons, break out the portable impact device—better known as a sledge hammer. It can get ugly, but you basically pound out the piston that has joined the cylinder wall.

Professional Mechanic Tip

37 Label Piston and Rod Assemblies

As the pistons and rods are removed from the block, it makes sense to label the pistons with tags, or mark them with a Sharpie to keep track of their original location in the block. If you are not going to reuse the pistons, there is no need to label them. With all the pistons and rods out of the engine, and front and rear main seals removed, the crank is about ready to vacate the block.

38 Lift Crankshaft From Block

Firmly grasp both ends of the crankshaft and lift it straight up and out of the journals. The crankshaft weighs about 70 pounds; you may want to have a friend help you. You don't want to drop it and injure yourself or damage the crank. Some of the bearing halves may be stuck to the crankshaft so be sure to remove them and properly mark them for the assembly process.

39 Remove Main Bearings

With the crank out of the block, the top half of the main bearings must be examined and removed. In order to remove the main bearings, place a screwdriver under the bearing, and then lift. Some bearings come right out, while others may need some penetrant lube and taps on the screwdriver to break them loose. Be very careful to avoid damaging the crank journal and the main bearing saddles.

When you examine the bearings, look for deep scars, gouges, discoloration, embedded particles, and overall condition of the bearing. This may indicate an existing problem with the engine that needs to be corrected during the rebuild. Use a small flathead screwdriver to pry out the rear main seal. You have to scrape the area clean to rid it of residue rubber from the seal.

40 Clean Up Cylinders

Attach a ball hone to a drill and run it through the cylinders, with plenty of WD-40 used to help with cleanup. Though this step is not necessary, you might want to get a better look at the cylinder walls to see if there is any obvious cracks or damage.

INSPECTION

Tearing apart an engine provides a great deal of excitement (or anxiety) about purchasing new parts. Seeing all those old, greasy parts organized in bags on your workbench might lead you to conclude that nothing can be reused. However, many parts can be reused for certain applications. Further, you might have lucked into buying an engine that had a recent overhaul, and a number of internal parts may have been barely used. Don't miss an opportunity to purchase a bargain engine from someone who is either abandoning an engine project or just couldn't get one to run right, but if you do buy a used engine it needs to be thoroughly inspected. This chapter includes information for determining the viability of an engine for a rebuild.

Inspection is dependent on good organization of parts as they were removed. If a compression check was performed prior to disassembly, look for particular problem areas/cylinders for clues. A compression check on a complete, running engine involves cleaning the area around the spark plugs with a wire brush and com-pressed air, removing all the spark plugs, blocking the throttle wide open, and detaching the coil wire (center wire) from the distributor and grounding it to the engine block using a jumper wire with clips. Screw the hose end of the compression gauge into the spark plug hole of cylinder number-1, and crank over the engine with six to eight compression strokes (the gauge reads the compression in psi). Test each cylinder the same way and record the numbers. Lower compression indicates problems with the head gaskets, pistons, piston rings, valves, or valve seats.

Much of the inspection process involves looking closely at your engine parts for signs of breakage or abnormal wear patterns. Be careful to look at the big picture rather than assuming a component simply failed because of defect. While this book cannot cover every single problem and cause, some common issues in failed engines are highlighted. For example, a broken and twisted connecting rod is more likely the result of a rod bolt failure than the connecting rod itself coming apart. A flattened cam lobe may have resulted from previous improper rebuilding

When you first drain the oil prior to disassembly, make sure to look in the oil for any metal filings, or metal fragments. Any pieces of metal could, but not always, mean bad news. Any milkiness in the oil could be an indicator of coolant collecting in the oil pan—a condition that could exist with a worn head gasket, cracked heads, or cracked cylinder block.

Removing the valve cover for the first time can be a moment of great disappointment or relief. In this case, there were mixed reviews. All the rockers, valvesprings, and pushrods seemed to be in place, but the parts were covered with sludge, suggesting a poorly maintained engine. The area where the rockers mount to the shaft was out of shape and thin, showing serious repair that called for the rocker arms to be replaced.

Check the Oil

A quick check of the oil provides some telltale signs of the health of the engine. If the oil is milky or somewhat lighter in color, it's possible coolant leaked into the engine oil, which could mean a blown head gasket or warped head. If metal particles or shavings are in the oil, some serious failure or metal-to-metal contact occurred. Rigorous investigation is required to identify the source of the problem that caused the engine failure and necessitated the engine rebuild.

Inspect the Cylinder Heads

The cylinder heads must use compatible rocker arm assemblies, valves, springs, retainers, and so forth. In addition, the cam must be compatible with the valvetrain; otherwise, the engine does not perform at its best. As you remove and disassemble the heads, look for cracks, unusual wear patterns, and any foreign matter that may have entered the combustion chamber. If the engine suffered a valve failure, it is plainly evident.

techniques or oiling failure. Foreign particles in the engine, overheating, and improper antifreeze/coolant protection in cold weather can all lead to breakage or premature wear.

A cylinder leak-down test can be performed if a compression test is not possible. The engine need not be complete or running for a leak-down test. Like the basic compression test, doing a cylinder leak-down test identifies problems with head gaskets, pistons, rings, valves, cracked heads, or cracked cylinder walls.

A leak-down test is performed by bringing cylinder number-1 to top dead center (TDC) on the compression stroke and pressurizing the cylinder with compressed air. An assistant is needed to make sure the crankshaft does not move when pressure fills the combustion chamber. The leak-down rate is measured by marking how much air escapes the cylinder. If 100 psi is pumped into the chamber, and the gauge reads 93 psi, you have a 7-percent leak-down rate. A rate of 10 percent is considered normal for a street engine, but a newly rebuilt street engine should be in the neighborhood of 2 percent or less.

A leak rate close to 20 percent means a rebuild is required. If air is heard coming through the exhaust manifolds, an exhaust valve is leaking. Air coming through the intake manifold or carburetor points to an intake valve leaking, whereas air heard coming from the crankcase points to blow-by past the pistons and rings.

General Inspection Procedure

1 Inspect Engine

This sludge buildup in the heads was a sign that the engine had likely not been apart in a long time, if ever. The sludge also was a tipoff that the oil had not been changed as often as it should have been. However, this type of sludge buildup could also be explained by the use of poor-quality oil. As a result, all of the rocker arms showed significant wear from the shaft, as well as on the tips of the rockers. The cam and lifter showed brown discoloration and the timing chain showed excessive play. The tops of the pistons had a solid layer of carbon buildup, all but eliminating the possibility of reusing them even for a stock street car rebuild.

Critical Inspection

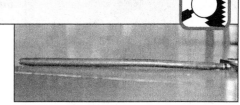

2 Inspect Pushrods

During disassembly, check the pushrods to see if they are loose, which indicates either a flattened cam lobe or a failing lifter. The pushrod itself could be bent, and misaligned, as well. Verify the straightness of the pushrods by rolling them across a piece of glass or truly flat surface. If a pushrod isn't straight, replace it.

After removing the pushrods, check them by laying them on a truly flat surface and rolling them along the surface. A bent pushrod is immediately apparent as it does not roll smoothly. You can roll the pushrods across a flat table or a piece of glass.

That is important to know if you are doing a budget rebuild and are attempting to reinstall the existing camshaft. If the pushrods are straight, both the lifters and pushrods could be usable after cleaning and further inspection. However, new cam and lifters are strongly recommended for even the tightest budgets.

Precision Measurement

3 Inspect Rocker Shaft Hole

Either this 1964 383-ci engine had seen many miles of service, or it was not receiving adequate lubrication. Note the side wear and thin metal around the rocker shaft hole. The heads are certainly salvageable, but the valvetrain components are in relatively poor condition. The rockers on this engine must be replaced with new units. The cylinder heads appear to be in good shape, though they certainly need to be rebuilt. Prior to that rebuild, they must be Magnafluxed to determine that they are free from cracks and damage. When you inspect your valvetrain components, examine the rockers closely, and if they are in good condition, which is possible, they must be kept in order so that they can be replaced the same way they came off the rocker assembly.

4 Measure Timing Chain Freeplay

The timing chain on this engine was extremely sloppy and clearly in need of replacement. Using a straight-edge along the middle of the chain, a measurement of more than .500 inch of slop calls for replacement. If your engine has not been rebuilt recently, replace the chain even if it is tight. It is cheap insurance for keeping your newly rebuilt engine together.

5 Inspect Timing Gear

Any engine rebuild requires a timing chain and timing gear replacement. This particular engine was long overdue for replacement. Notice the severe wear on the timing chain gear.

6 Inspect Lifters

The lifter faces should be perfectly flat, unlike this one. There shouldn't be any cracks, pits, or other damage. Years of use have created pro- nounced wear, the death sentence for this set of lifters. If you identify some damage, replace the lifter.

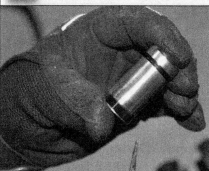

Use a straightedge (not shown) or another method to do a basic check of the pressure required to compress the lifter. If you have access to a simple press, use it to check the lifters. If the lifters are to be re-used, make sure they all compress under equal pressure.

8 Inspect Dampener

Rubber built into an OEM vibration dampener can sometimes begin to deteriorate or bulge out of the seam, which indicates it's time for replacement. Don't overlook the importance of a dampener in building an engine that is free from vibrations. An extensive rebuild that includes a new rotating assembly calls for careful selection of a replacement dampener from a reputable source.

9 Inspect Cylinder Heads

Rather than spending money on cylinder heads that are suspect, carefully examine them before they are sent off to be hot tanked and Magnafluxed or sonically checked. Check the head gaskets to see if the head appears to properly seal to the block. Look in the ports to see if there is any oily residue or rust that could lead to cracks in the valve seats or the head itself. Make sure there are no marks in the combustion chamber from the piston hitting the head. Carefully examine all surfaces for cracks, deformations, and other damage. Check also for valve marks in the piston from the valve hitting the top of the piston at high RPM; this indicates a valvetrain failure.

Important!

9 Inspect Cylinder Heads CONTINUED

Disassemble and Magnaflux the cylinder heads to check for any cracks. In a Magnaflux test, a powerful magnet magnetizes the cast-iron head and a fine dust of particles is spread through the combustion chamber and other areas of the head. The powder adheres to the walls and surfaces of the head and collects in any cracks or deformations, thus revealing these problems. Initial inspection of this engine showed that the valves have common wear for their age and mileage, but they will be replaced.

Cylinder head disassembly is necessary to check the valves more carefully. As the valves are removed, the keeper grooves and hardware must be examined. Scoring, uneven wear, discoloration, and carbon buildup can occur when the valveguide leaks and allows oil to enter the intake port. Replace the valves when those maladies occur. Upon removal, the valvestems should be checked for wear and valvestem-to-guide clearance.

Also check to see if the springs are square by placing them on a flat surface. Place a combination square on top of the spring. Rotate the spring, and check for unevenness or gaps. If you have access to a valvespring load tester, get the load capacity of the spring from the spring manufacturer. You can also measure spring free height with a vernier caliper to see if it matches spec, or simply compare the springs to one another to detect variations in height. Anything more than .0625-inch difference in height calls for spring replacement.

Carbon buildup in the combustion chambers often results in detonation. Detonation is the explosion of the fuel charge at the wrong time in the four-stroke cycle and/or spontaneous ignition of unburned air/fuel mixture. Preignition is the premature explosion of the air/fuel mixture in the chamber prior to the spark plug igniting the mixture. Preignition and detonation are usually called pinging, which you might hear when your vehicle seeks to maintain speed while traversing an incline.

Critical Inspection

10 Inspect Pistons

Significant carbon buildup on the tops of these pistons was no surprise. Even though they will be replaced, you need to know which piston came out of which cylinder. Excellent diagnostic information can be gained from keeping track of each piston's location. For example, if cylinder number-4 is severely scratched or scarred, a close look at piston number-4 may give an explanation of the problem. Either oil starvation or piston ring failure are the likely culprits.

Critical Inspection

11 Examine Camshaft

Examine the camshaft journals for wear, grooves, or gouges. Inspect the lobes for any abnormal wear patterns, deep scratches, or scoring. (Of course, if you've decided to buy a new cam with different timing, this is unnecessary.) A typical wear pattern on the lobe should be wider at the nose of the lobe and narrower at the heel. This particular cam shows a wider pattern of wear that extends to the side of the lobe, somewhat indicative of more severe wear. Either poor lubrication or a lot of miles led to the condition of this cam, and the result is that it needs to be replaced. If the camshaft exhibits abnormal or severe wear, it should be replaced.

If you're doing a strictly stock build, you can opt for a cam with stock timing. If you're building a modified engine, the cam's lift, duration, and timing needs to match the valvetrain and heads you select. And of course, if a problem led to the destruction of the cam, the source of the problem needs to be identified and corrected.

12 Replace Oil Pump

Replace your oil pump during the rebuild because a new pump is inexpensive, and therefore, rebuilding the old one makes little sense. You can check for metal pieces or shavings in the old one and if you are curious as to whether it was properly functioning, place it in a container of solvent and spin its drive-shaft. A few revolutions should result in some evidence of flow.

Inspect the Crankshaft

The crankshaft is subjected to an enormous amount of stress over its lifetime. Closely examine the crankshaft journals for scratches, marring, or any other damage. Measure the crankshaft journals to ensure they haven't been turned down or resurfaced. If they have, new bearings are needed to accommodate the crankshaft. Also check runout to be sure that the crank is straight enough for the rebuild. If it is found to be out of specification, take it to a machine shop to be straightened.

1 Measure Crankshaft Endplay

Crankshaft endplay is the distance a crankshaft can move forward or backward in the block. One of the best diagnostic methods for inspecting an engine is to measure crank endplay as the engine is being disassembled. The factory crankshaft endplay tolerance is .002 to .007 inch. On the big-block Mopar, main bearing cap number-3 is the thrust bearing. If it is worn, it indicates that the crankshaft is not true or a bearing failure occurred.

2 Measure Endplay

Position a dial indicator on the snout of the crank to measure crankshaft endplay. With the dial indicator in place, use a large screwdriver to gently pry the crankshaft forward and backward. This crank endplay measured .007 inch, within the factory tolerance of .002 to .007. Any more than that indicates thrust bearing wear.

Critical Inspection

3 Rod Inspection

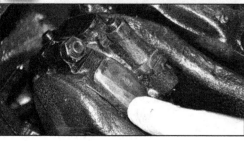

The connecting rods are one of the most-heavily stressed parts in the engine. High mileage can easily produce metal fatigue, and even hairline cracks in the rods. Although this build features reconditioned stock rods, I would have preferred to replace the original rods with aftermarket units. Note that this engine's rods appear to have been re-balanced. They do not look factory, so the engine might have had a spun bearing, necessitating removal and replacement of the rod and bearing shells.

4 Inspect Crankshaft

The grind marks around the oil hole in the crank show that this crank might have received some grinding work to enlarge the oil hole, but it could have occurred at the factory. A spun bearing could have been the reason for chamfering the oil hole on that journal.

This factory forged-steel crank has been removed and will be sent to Jim Lewis' crankshaft specialist. But before that happens, a basic visual inspection must be made. Remove the thrust bearing and check its condition. Check the crank journals for damage, specifically deep grooves or discoloration. Minor wear can be remedied when the crank is sent out to be cut. The good reading on the crank endplay gave a good indication of this thrust bearing's fair condition.

5 Inspect Crankshaft Journals

All B low-deck big-block Mopars share a crankshaft journal size of 2.625 inches. The RB raised-deck big-block Chryslers have a 2.750-inch journal size. Use a micrometer to take a measurement that gives you an indication of whether the crank is virgin or it has been reground. Any discoloration on the crankshaft journals is cause for concern because this indicates bearing wear or some type of oil starvation. Inspect the oil holes in the crank to see if they are clogged, or if they have received some type of unorthodox modifications. Check the journals with a dial indicator to see if there is excessive taper or out-of-round condition. This particular crankshaft was found to be in good shape, useable after being reground. Make sure the crank snout is undamaged, and that the keyway is still intact.

The crank journals should be smooth and have a consistent finish. A damaged journal may have grooves or other surface damage from being improperly handled. Improper installation with insufficient or excessive bearing crush can cause bearing failure. Insufficient lubrication or overheating can lead to bearing failure. A twisted connecting rod or main bearing cap shift also leads to main bearing stress and failure. Foreign particles from dirty oil can lead to scoring and gouging of the bearing surface.

Inspect the Cylinder Block

The engine block is the foundation of your engine build. The fact that your engine was running prior to disassembly does not guarantee that it is a good candidate for rebuilding. Visual inspection includes looking for signs of overheating, excessive gasket sealer from previous repairs, a leaking water pump, or core plugs that are leaking. Also check for obvious cracks and indications of core shift, mounting holes for external components like the fuel pump and oil pump, and the oil pan rail for cracks or breakage. A pressure check and magnaflux inspection by your machinist is the only way to be confident of the integrity of the block.

1 Inspect Rear Main Seal

Remove the rear main seal if it is severely worn. If the rear main seal is fused to the groove, it must be scraped out with a small screwdriver. A small scraper does the job easily.

2 Inspect Main Bearing Caps

Inspect main caps for any cracks or damage. After removing the main caps, inspect the main bearings for excessive wear. Visually inspect the bearings for uneven thickness, big gouges, severe scratches, or "trenches" in the bearing surface. Don't worry about small scratches, but if you drag a penny across the bearing and the scratches can be felt, wear is likely excessive and calls for replacement.

Inspect the bearings for blue discoloration from oil starvation. A milky gray or black corrosion on the lining could indicate water or antifreeze in the oil. Worn or pitted surfaces with dark green discoloration may reveal the presence of fuel dilution of the oil, which could also have damaged the crankshaft. Examine for spots or foreign particles embedded in the bearing. All these conditions require bearing replacement.

3 Examine Block

Before doing any work on the block, measure each cylinder and determine if it has been overbored previously. The consensus is that a stock block is good to .060 overbore—any bigger bore than that risks failure. Another way to determine if a block has any hope of being usable is to check the cam tunnel for core shift. A visible check certainly is reassuring, but a sonic test is the best method.

Using a sonic tester, the machinist at a machine shop is able to determine the cylinder wall thickness and whether the cylinder meets minimal thickness tolerances. If the cylinders walls are thinner at the bottom of the bore, the block is most likely useable because the cylinder is under the most stress at the top of the bore where the combustion process occurs. This Chrysler 383 block shows virtually no core shift, as the material around the tunnel is equal.

As with the heads, Magnaflux the block because you need a solid foundation for your engine rebuild. If there are cracks on the main bearing saddles or in the webbing area, your block is probably not worth rebuilding. Have the machine shop do a Magnaflux test or perform one at home to determine that the block is sound.

4 Sonically Test Block

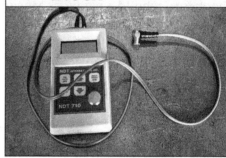

This NDT 710 sonic tester sends sound waves through the block, heads, and other components to determine the thickness of the castings. Engine builders can accurately determine the thickness of the metal surrounding each of the cylinder bores, main bearing saddles, and critical areas in the cylinder heads. If the components are within the factory spec, they are suitable for a rebuild.

5 Clean Cylinder Walls

After the crank, rods, and pistons have been removed from the short block, use a stone cylinder brush with a liberal amount of cleaning solvent to clean the cylinder walls and get them ready for boring. Lewis said, "This block looks to be in good shape; it won't clean up at thirty [.030 inch], but it will clean up at sixty [.060 inch]."

PARTS SELECTION

The focus of this *Workbench®* book is to rebuild a big-block Mopar that makes about 300 or more horsepower or for a high-performance rebuild using the stock block to produce up to 600 hp. To make 600 hp, you cannot rely on OEM parts.

Instead, you must use aftermarket parts. In fact, to rebuild a Mopar big-block that produces more than 600 hp, you need aftermarket heads, crank, connecting rods, and block, which is outside the scope of this book. In this chapter, I show you the variety of stock components for a Mopar big-block B or RB engine, and build a very respectable package.

Any engine rebuild plan ultimately boils down to three simple questions. First, what is your application? If you are doing a basic rebuild for a street car, and are simply interested in restoring the engine to its former performance levels, the parts, machining processes, and assembly procedures are vastly different from a performance-oriented rebuild. This basic rebuild is certainly less expensive, and a bit simpler, as well.

Second, how much horsepower do you want to make? In the case of an old Mopar B or RB block, you may want more than a stock rebuild with a step up in the camshaft and valvetrain departments. In the search for more horsepower, greater fuel economy, or more impressive idle for cruise nights, substantial increases in power call for a more meticulous rebuild. Others are looking for the greatest horsepower increase possible for a wild show car, dedicated race car, or even some kind of off-road beast.

In this chapter, the goal is to show you a variety of stock components for a Mopar Big Block B or RB engine, as well as some basic aftermarket parts, which can come together to create a very respectable performance package while remaining under the 600-hp ceiling. Stock exhaust manifolds provide trouble-free operation for the street driver. They are quiet, bolt right up to replacement exhaust systems, and rarely leak or fail. They are easy to work with during engine removal and can usually remain on the engine. On the other hand, stock cast-iron exhaust manifolds restrict exhaust scavenging. One of the greatest performance improvements that can be made to an engine is to install a properly designed, free-flowing exhaust system. If you desire improved performance, you will see good results by ditching your stock exhaust manifolds in favor of a quality set of headers.

Third, how much do you want to spend? An engine with a spun bearing might be a good candidate for a "rings and bearings" job, which can be accomplished for less than $2,000. Rather than going through all the trouble of expensive machining and parts purchases, rebuilding a tired 440 sitting in an old farm truck might drive the frugal owner to do the minimally required work to get that RB engine running again. But be warned, that approach to engine building might cost more in the long run.

A more realistic view of a proper bone-stock engine rebuild focuses on economy and reliability costs $3,000 to $4,000. Stepping up to a strong street performance engine should cost anywhere from $5,000 to $10,000, depending on the machining and assembly processes demanded and the cost of aftermarket performance parts. Although beyond the scope of this book, climbing the break-the-budget ladder, a state-of-the-art, trick-of-the-month race car engine can easily cost $20,000 or more. As choices are made to purchase parts,

seek input from experienced engine builders in order to develop an integrated parts package that produces optimum results. It also makes sense to consider using software, such as Comp Cams' Desktop Dyno ($50), to guide you in the selection of parts. It enables you to enter data for your particular engine, set criteria for your application, give options for product choices, and then predict horsepower levels. Comp Cams also offers a free download of its CamQuest 6 software, which makes it simple to select a camshaft and predict power levels with a number of both stock and aftermarket components that are readily available.

Rebuilding a Stock Engine

A bone-stock, or strictly stock, rebuild is suitable for many cars and owners. Many people have a limited budget, and want to build an engine that provides reliable service for a minimum amount of dollars. The budget build requires paying careful attention to disassembly and inspection proce-

dures, so as many parts as possible can be reused for the rebuild with a minimum number of parts replaced.

For example, if the cylinders show little or no wear, larger bore pistons would not need to be purchased. However, pistons must be inspected for condition and size. Scored or damaged pistons need to be replaced. Many purists who are involved in a concours-correct restoration often prefer to do as little surgery to their numbers-correct engines as possible. Careful inspection determines if an engine could be restored to good power and reliability levels with a simple hone job and replacement of rings, rod bearings, main bearings, freeze plugs, and gaskets.

A number of sources for rebuild kits are surprisingly affordable, especially with the more recent advent of parts from overseas suppliers. Some complain about the reality of parts not made in America (I'm one of them), but there is no denying that the cheaper parts have made it possible for some on limited funds to enjoy the hobby.

Competition Products offers a basic engine rebuild package of rings, bearings, and gaskets starting at about $85. Of course, you can be penny-wise and pound foolish when rebuilding an engine. So unless funds are nonexistent, a minimal recommended rebuild is to step up to Competition Products Master Rebuild Kit, which includes flat-top pistons, matching piston rings, rod, main and cam bearings, standard volume oil pump, complete gasket set, freeze plug kit, cam and lifters, and a three piece timing set. It sells for about for $250 (at the time of this writing).

Rebuild kits can be upgraded to include a fully balanced rotating assembly, with higher quality parts

Many purists involved in a concours-correct restoration often prefer to do as little surgery to their numbers-correct engines as possible. Careful inspection may determine that an engine could be restored to good power and reliability levels with a simple hone job and replacement of rings, rod bearings, main bearings, freeze plugs, and gaskets. There are a number of affordable rebuild kits, such as Summit's basic rings, bearings, and gasket kit for a 383 Chrysler for less than $300. Upgraded with forged pistons, an oil pump, and better rings, you can still get a rebuild kit from Summit for about $800. The prices increase with higher quality parts, but you do not have to break the bank to rebuild your engine.

Premium Parts for Racing

Given the number of rules and restrictions involved in building a Stock Eliminator engine, building a car with competitive power is a serious challenge. The engine must be reliable even though it runs many OEM components. The engine must feature a light reciprocating mass even while running stock connecting rods and NHRA-specified weight for rod and piston assembly. Recognizing that an engine is simply a big air pump, the engine must be able to breathe properly even though the stock carb, cam lift, and heads are OEM spec. The engine must be built to produce the torque necessary to get the relatively heavy race car down the quarter-mile in the 11-second range. Quick math says that a mid-11-second run in a 3,700-pound car is going to take almost 500 hp from an engine that is NHRA rated at 280 hp.

How do these stocker engines achieve 1.5 hp per cubic inch within said parameters? Overall, the approach is to build an engine that produces a lot of torque. In Jim Lewis' words, "Torque gets it going, horsepower keeps it going." Drag cars must be built to optimize torque production in the RPM band in which they typically function. The best powerband is absolutely crucial to understand how to assemble the right parts for the optimum performance in the quarter-mile. Essentially, the challenge is met through a loose rotating assembly, cylinder pressure, cam duration, and maximum airflow.

Most aftermarket blocks have built-in advantages over OEM blocks, such as a stronger main bearing web, thicker cylinder walls, and any number of design enhancements so the block can handle much more horsepower. But, those advantages are not necessary for an engine that is projected to remain under 600 hp. Of course, there is no guarantee that an OEM-block, 500-hp engine will be indestructible. However, after my years of Super Stock racing with OEM blocks, it's safe to say that when properly machined, OEM B and RB blocks are typically adequate for up to 600 hp.

available for higher cost. If your project is a four-door midsize that will not see duty above 4,000 rpm, these parts are more than sufficient for your application. Quite honestly, many older restored cars are rarely exercised above 3,000 rpm, making moly rings, forged pistons, and high-dollar connecting rods unnecessary.

Rebuilding a Strong Street Engine

The biggest mistake on most street engines, other than assembly errors, is the temptation to run too much camshaft. There is no denying that an engine with a big cam and compatible parts usually brings a big high-RPM number. However, for spirited street driving, big torque numbers bring the best seat-of-the-pants performance increase. If you are performing a strictly stock rebuild, use a cam with the factory lift, duration, lobe separation, and other specs; but if you want to increase performance, select a cam with high-performance timing events. That requires careful research and selection of all val-

vetrain components to ensure that the cam and all related components are compatible and complementary (aspects to consider for buying a cam are discussed on page 58). A properly matched engine component kit takes into account the expected driving conditions. Everyone loves the big, rumpety cam for cruise nights, but a smaller cam that delivers in the lower RPM range typically makes for a better street engine.

Stroker kits are especially effective in producing the torque needed for street conditions. The Mopar B and especially RB engines with their healthy deck height blocks make them excellent candidates for increasing the engine's stroke in order to gain displacement.

OEM Main Caps

The B and RB engines use five cast-iron two-bolt main caps. They are numbered one to five front to rear, and must be returned to their proper locations. Both the B and RB blocks with stock main caps cannot withstand much more than about 600 hp. Broken main caps and cracks in the main web are areas with high potential for failure. Hard block, girdles, aluminum main caps, and cross-bolted four-bolt main caps are all available from the aftermarket to strengthen factory blocks. The general consensus

from engine builders is that the factory main caps are sufficient for an engine making less than 600 hp.

Aftermarket Two-Bolt Main Caps

Most engine builders use OEM iron two-bolt main caps in the B and RB Mopar big-blocks because they are more than adequate to keep the bottom end together, even for 7,000-plus-rpm blasts. This type of engine build features the OEM two-bolt main caps using ARP main cap bolts. The use of ARP bolts over stock main cap bolts changes the installation torque spec from 85 to 100 ft-lbs.

As power levels go above the 600-hp mark, bottom-end instability results in a condition called "cap walk," which can lead to cracks and

breakage in the main webs of the block.

Whether the goal is peace of mind or future power upgrades, some owners upgrade their engine's bottom end with aftermarket two-bolt main caps made of either aluminum or steel. (Mancini Racing offers a two-bolt aluminum main bearing cap that's ideal for high-horsepower builds.)

Some believe the aluminum main cap upgrade allows the crank to flex slightly without suffering breakage, acting similar to a shock absorber. A big-block Mopar in the 800-hp range causes the crank to want to exit the bottom of the block, so as the aluminum takes some of the hit from the crank, the main bearings move around slightly. That movement shortens bearing life, and ultimately leads to bearing failure or breakage. A

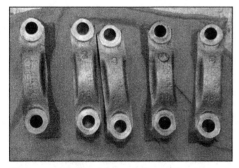

The stock two-bolt main caps were used in this build, and are numbered from the factory for proper location. Options for main caps are available from the aftermarket, and preferred by some engine builders. Many recommend aftermarket two-bolt aluminum main caps, such as those available from Mancini Racing. Other builders prefer billet-steel two-bolt main caps, such as those available from 440Source. Pro-Gram offers four-bolt main caps, which require modifications to the sides of the block for a cross-bolt arrangement

Carefully select and order the correct bearings for your engine; remember that the B low-deck blocks (361, 383, 400) have a smaller crankshaft journal diameter than the RB (413, 426, 440) engines. In addition, the 1974-and-newer blocks incorporate a larger thrust bearing than the earlier blocks, so make sure you specify your exact year and engine size.

Concerning various materials used for main bearings, Clevite offers a standard BiMetal bearing that is well-suited for standard rebuilds. The BiMetal moniker is a reference to the 100-percent lead-free aluminum silicon bi-metal material and is undoubtedly a fine standard rebuild bearing. But I advise you to step up to Clevite 77 TriMetal engine bearings. Clevite offers H, P, and V TriMetal bearing types. The type you need depends on your application and usage.

Generally speaking, an H-bearing features enlarged chamfers for greater crankshaft filet clearance and is designed for a medium-range-RPM engine, like a strong street stroker engine that is not likely to exceed 5,500 to 6,000 rpm.

The P bearing is designed for higher RPM usage, so Jim Lewis ordered the fully grooved P bearings that worked with my 383 Stock Eliminator engine running the reground B engine OEM crankshaft. The P bearing has a protective coating for initial startup. Fully grooved bearings get mixed reviews, because some say that you don't need the full groove or it's a waste of oil. With a 60-psi Melling oil pump, there is plenty of oil pressure available for the grooved bearings.

steel main cap, especially when complemented by a girdle, is a better alternative to the aluminum main cap, as it provides a more rigid bottom end.

Four-Bolt Main Conversion

Big-block Mopar engines can be converted from two-bolt mains to four-bolt mains using an aftermarket cross-bolted main conversion. However, many feel there is not enough material in the main webs to support a four-bolt main cap conversion, and you cannot convert the front and rear bearing caps to a four-bolt configuration.

Converting it requires precise drilling into the pan rail of the block. Drilling holes into the pan rail of a two-bolt main block, in my opinion, only introduces six new places for the block to crack. For that reason, I don't recommend the conversion. If power numbers are expected to be north of 600 hp, and a four-bolt main block is desired, purchase a Keith Black, World Products, or Koleno Performance block that is cast with provisions for cross-bolted mains, and call it a day.

ARP Rod Bolts and Main Cap Bolts

Rod bolts are an area where strength is absolutely essential. ARP offers three lines of rod bolts suited for various applications. ARP's standard high-performance rod bolts are made of premium-grade 8740 alloy chrome-moly steel, which is heat treated to provide a tensile strength in the 200,000-psi range. ARP's own tests show these bolts to be five times more reliable than stock bolts.

The next step up is the ARP Wave-Loc high-performance rod bolts. Using the same heat-treated 8740 alloy chrome-moly steel, these rod bolts feature a shank design with symmetrical waves that provide a tight fit in the rod without creating

Engine builder Jim Lewis put it succinctly, "If I have the option of starting from scratch to build the best engine I can build, then I want CP Pistons." There's good reason for Jim's preference. CP forgings are computer designed for superior strength and light weight, and CNC machined for the highest standards of accuracy. CP employs a technique called "maximum internal lightening," a process of removing weight from the piston without compromising its integrity and reliability.

One of the great benefits of CP Pistons is the up-to-the-minute technology in the piston and Total Seal ring package. The Total Seal ring package is loaded with trick technology and features a groove in the spacer of the top ring assembly. That groove allows combustion gases to enter behind the top ring and improves ring seal by forcing the ring against the cylinder wall during combustion.

For a big-block Mopar producing less than 600 hp, the OEM forged crankshaft is up to the task in both strength and reliability. Companies such as Callies and Ohio have excellent reputations with engine builders. However, an aftermarket crankshaft for this rebuild would be a waste of money.

Mopar supplied two connecting rod lengths for the B and RB engines. The low-block B engines (350, 361, 383, and 400 ci) came equipped with 6.358-inch connecting rods. The RB engines had a 6.768-inch connecting rod (PN 16116). The 1970 to 1971 440 6-barrel RB engines came equipped with a stout, heavy-duty rod (PN 2951906), which was also found in the 1971 to 1973 440 high-performance engine.

the stress risers commonly found in bolts that have a knurl. Simply stated, galling and scoring of the rod is virtually eliminated because there is only smooth contact with the rod.

The Wave-Loc technology is applied to ARP's third line, the Pro Series Wave-Loc rod bolts. This type is intended for the most severe applications and perfect for aftermarket rods. Pro Series Wave-Loc bolts are made from a material that ARP calls ARP2000. According to the company, this material has approximately twice the fatigue life of 8740 chrome-moly steel and a tensile strength of about 220,000 psi with a capability of 12,000 pounds of clamping force.

Aftermarket Rods

Connecting rods are subjected to enormous stresses and take the brunt of the combustion forces. Be sure to select an excellent-quality rod for a strong, reliable engine. Connecting rod failure leads to outright engine failure and often destroys a block, pan, and other parts. High-quality aftermarket connecting rods in H- and I-beam configurations for B/RB engines are available from Hale Performance Sales (HPS), Carillo, Eagle, Manley, and Childs & Albert.

Both types of aftermarket rods offer comparable if not superior strength when compared to stock. H-beam rods are typically used for max-performance builds of more than 700 hp. I-beam rods are the most suitable for the type of build covered in this book. Typically, the aftermarket rods offer more reinforcement near the journal.

In addition to H- and I-beam configuration, rods are constructed of forged steel, aluminum, and cast iron. Aluminum is suitable for all-out racing engines due to low weight and limited service life. A cast rod is suitable for a low-300-hp build. A high-quality forged steel is the most suitable option for an engine up to 600 hp because of overall strength and long service life.

Rods must be checked for weight, tolerances, and overall condition. A new set of rods can be purchased for about the same money it takes to recondition a set of stock connecting rods. Many aftermarket rods are of excellent quality, but do your homework and ask around for recommendations from other engine builders.

No matter which rods you end up purchasing, make sure they are checked for flaws, and weighed to see if they are within tolerances. Most engine builders are comfortable working with rods that show quality of workmanship, arrive in the box within 1 gram of one another, and have gained a reputation for reliability.

The best NHRA-approved connecting rod for my B 383 engine is the Hale Performance Sales rod (PN 14199HPS), which is capable of handling up to 1,500 hp. That rod will be in my Super Stock engine that I hope to build in two years.

Pistons

Factory pistons from Mopar have either been cast aluminum or higher-performance forged aluminum. Some people simply want to leave the block alone, and it may not require overboring. Therefore, it may just need a cylinder hone with new rings and bearings as per the recommendation of your machine shop, plus a very nice cleanup of the existing pistons. That can make a lot of sense for budget purposes. Not only do you save on the cost of a new set of pistons, but machine shop costs are reduced by not having to bore the cylinders.

In addition to cast and forged pistons, hypereutectic pistons are considered a mid-range option. KB Pistons makes hypereutectic pistons, which offer some help in durability for the 325- to 400-hp-range engine. Anything more than 400 hp dictates the use of a forged piston. That horsepower range seems a bit narrow to justify a hypereutectic piston. Most cases that can be made for a "stepup" to the hypereutectic piston can ultimately make the case for simply buying a set of forged pistons.

OEM Pistons

If you re-use your original pistons from the engine, spend some time cleaning and scrubbing them before installation. This process is tedious, but as mentioned earlier, is preferable for the muscle car owner who is picky and determined to retain as many of the OEM parts as possible. If the choice is to stick with the factory pistons, consider a process called Zyglo—a liquid fluorescent penetrant system that reveals any cracks in aluminum parts such as factory pistons.

High-Performance Street Pistons

Select pistons that are compatible with the heads on your engine. A closed-chamber 915 is compatible with closed-chamber pistons, while an open-chamber piston is specifically made for an open-chamber head. So before you decide on that trick new forged piston, do the research to find out which pistons are compatible with which heads.

Piston rings provide a seal between the cylinder wall and the piston. If the piston rings are installed properly, they accurately regulate the amount of oil on the cylinder walls, aid in transferring heat from the combustion chamber to the block, and provide the suction that draws the fuel/air mixture into the combustion chamber. A ring package consists of three rings, the top compression ring, the second compression ring (which has been shown to be more about oil scraping than compression sealing), and the third ring (which scrapes the oil from the cylinder walls). A piston ring package affects the manner in which your engine builder finishes the cylinder wall, and how long a break-in period your newly rebuilt engine needs.

Cast iron, ductile iron, or stainless steel are the three types of piston ring materials. Basic, uncoated cast-iron rings break in quickly, but they do not last as long as other rings. A wise upgrade is to go with a package that features ductile iron and moly coating for the top compression ring. The higher quality moly-coated ductile-iron top ring is better able to withstand the heat of combustion, and it is the choice of many engine builders. The second ring is typically a standard cast-iron material, while the third oil ring is typically a three-piece arrangement, which is made of stainless steel.

Rings can be molybdenum faced, which aids the cylinder wall in retaining a greater amount of oil, thus making them last longer. Some piston rings can feature chrome plating or even ceramic coatings.

For oil supply, not much exotic is available or necessary. A standard-volume Melling oil pump is all that is required for a street-oriented rebuild.

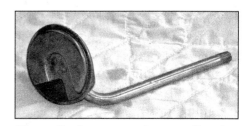

Mopar Performance also supplies the pickup for the 5-quart OEM-design oil pan. The pickup is threaded for ease of installation, but must be carefully positioned to ensure optimum effectiveness in delivering the oil supply. An improperly installed oil pickup can be disastrous to your newly rebuilt engine, resulting in oil starvation, and damage to rings, bearings, and cylinder walls, and eventually complete engine failure.

For basic stock rebuilds, an aftermarket dampener is not necessary unless the existing dampener is worn or shows signs of needing replacement. The typical operating range for a stock engine rarely exceeds 5,000 rpm, certainly within the ability of the OEM dampener to minimize torsional vibration.

With a solid reputation of many years, an ATI Damper is helpful in both high-performance street and race applications. If your street engine never revs higher than 5,000 rpm, the stock balancer suffices. But if you ever spin that Mopar more than 5,000 rpm, you need to step up to a compatible aftermarket dampener, such as an ATI Super Damper.

Don't go drag racing with your 40-year-old harmonic balancer, as that is clearly stone-age technology. With all the effort to balance the rotating assembly in your engine, the last thing you want is to deal with unwanted vibrations, which could lead to premature wear, and even catastrophic failure.

Mopar Performance offers good 5-quart stock oil pans. An upgrade includes a stock Hemi oil pan and pickup, which increases oil capacity from 5 to 6 quarts. A Chenoweth scraper keeps oil off the crank, and a good supply in the pan for uninterrupted lubrication reduces windage loss.

Pistons are available in cast, hypereutectic, and forged constructions. For a stock performance engine, a stock cast piston is adequate. However, if you rebuild an engine with higher horsepower, hypereutectic or forged pistons are the best options. A forged piston expands and contracts under running conditions, and therefore owners often experience piston slap when the engine is cold. Piston slap is not a common condition for hypereutectic pistons, which exhibit less expansion, but these pistons are not suitable for high-horsepower or power adders such as superchargers or nitrous oxide.

Many manufacturers provide forged pistons at affordable prices. For example, CP Pistons has recently introduced its line of Bullet Pistons. The great thing about the CP Bullet forged piston is that it is manufactured the same way as the more expensive pistons, from the same 2618 alloy, built with many of the same features, but simply more affordable.

Cylinder Heads

Care should be taken in the selection of cylinder heads. Since you've determined that the engine needs to be rebuilt, Magnaflux or sonically test your OEM stock heads in order to check for cracks. Should you buy another set of used cast-iron heads or a reconditioned set of heads from an aftermarket supplier? Possibly, but you might be considering an upgrade to an aftermarket aluminum head. For this rebuild, I was able to locate a set of stock, virgin, 915 castings for $300. They turned out to be excellent for my application, especially since they had the NHRA-spec 1.60 exhaust valve.

Consider the options and decide whether the cost and effort to rebuild a good set of heads is worth it. Where one person might enjoy the challenge of finding a suitable pair of OEM-core cylinder heads, another enthusiast may opt for the instant horsepower of a quality aftermarket head. If you opt for the aftermarket cylinder heads, make sure to purchase a set of heads that either have some sort of return policy or have already been checked for cracks.

OEM Cylinder Heads

The 383 engine project in this book is built around a set of cylinder heads that were optimized by Jim Lewis. Jim spent many hours testing the cylinder head airflow on a flowbench. It provides exact CFM numbers of how much air/fuel mixture each port is able to accommodate.

The decision to stick with the OEM cast-iron heads or go with a pair of aftermarket heads is an important one. Most aftermarket heads are aluminum, and the choices are numerous. For many applications, buying an aftermarket cylinder head costs about the same as reconditioning the stock heads. Consider your usage, budget,

and ultimate performance goals when selecting cylinder heads.

Since this engine is a race engine governed by NHRA rules, increased airflow is accomplished by completing a multi-angle a valve job and perfecting valve fitment.

Increasing airflow into an engine increases performance. In 1966, 383 engines typically came with 516 casting heads. Though these heads can be made to work in Super Stock, they leave a lot to be desired for Stock Eliminator. Jim Hale to the rescue— he worked with NHRA to legalize the much better 915 casting heads with the 2.08 intake and 1.60 exhaust valves.

Aftermarket Cylinder Heads

The aluminum Edelbrock Performer RPM head was the first "bolt on and go" head. It is compatible with a stock block and provides far better flow than a stock head. RPM heads have a 2.140-inch intake valve and a 1.81-inch exhaust valve, which are larger than stock. This aftermarket head is a suitable option for a high-performance street engine.

For street duty under 5,500 rpm, the affordable E Street aluminum heads offer strong performance. Performer RPM aluminum heads offer bigger torque and horsepower numbers up to 6,500 rpm, while the Victor and Victor CNC heads are designed for racing. Other vendors also offer products worthy of consideration for your engine build, such as Brodix, Indy, 440Source, and Mopar Performance.

It is important to consider the price involved in rebuilding your old head; it could get very close to the price of a new head. Make sure that the heads have provisions for all your accessories (especially if you building a street engine). A bolt-on aftermarket cylinder head likely means that it fits your block, not that every last accessory bracket is accommodated on the new head. Further, make sure that any cylinder head you buy works with the rest of your engine package.

Camshaft and Valvetrain

A common mistake made in parts selection is choosing a cam that is too big, with either too much lift or too much duration. The thinking is fairly simple—more cam equals more power, but it's not that simple. An engine must be built as an entire package, and that axiom is especially true when considering camshaft choice. The cowboy mentality of a guy building a street engine is to listen to his builder's advice on cams, but then bump it up a notch or two wilder.

There are four types of cams from which to choose: mechanical flat tappet, hydraulic flat tappet, mechanical roller cam, and hydraulic roller cam. The four designations relate to the type of lifter that is used, and that choice impacts the cam profile. A mechanical (more commonly called solid-lifter) cam was used in a number of big-block engines from

1962 to 1964, including the Max Wedge engines. The 1965-and-later big-block engines came with hydraulic lifter cams. If you are looking for strong street performance or want a street car that can run healthy ETs, a hydraulic roller cam can be an excellent way to bring those two worlds together. If you are building a race engine, you probably want to think about a mechanical roller cam. Many modern OEM performance cars are built with hydraulic roller cams and lifters.

The camshaft is the one component in the engine that affects almost every other decision. An honest appraisal of how your vehicle is going to be used is key to proper camshaft selection. A mild camshaft exactly like the one that came in your car from the manufacturer is a good choice for exclusive street duty. Some cams are very similar in character to stock, but benefit from slightly higher torque production. Many people refer to a higher-torque cam as an RV cam. The guy who occasionally wants to smoke his tires appreciates a higher-torque street cam with good drivability manners. In most street-duty cam selections,

the rest of the OEM valvetrain components are sufficient, especially the B/RB engines with their factory shaft rocker assemblies.

A solid-lifter cam is often used as a high-performance street or race cam. In the past, running a solid-lifter cam on the street typically required frequent valve adjustment, but adjustable rocker assemblies can reduce the amount of maintenance required for solid lifters.

A hydraulic flat-tappet cam requires little if any maintenance as it is flogged on the street. However, the high-performance street engine greatly benefits from a hydraulic roller cam, allowing more aggressive cam profiles with excellent reliability. Not surprisingly, a roller cam and roller lifter package is more expensive than a standard hydraulic cam and lifter package.

Before you buy, talk to the cam manufacturers, and let them know what kind of driving and usage your engine will be getting.

Aftermarket Cams

A typical camshaft manufacturer offers a number of different camshaft lines depending on application. For flat-tappet street engines, Comp Cams offers Magnum Cams, High Energy Cams, and Xtreme Energy cams. Drag racers have been using Sportsman/Bracket Comp Cams for years in both solid-lifter flat-tappet and solid-lifter roller-cam designs. For those longing for drive-in hero status with a big, lopey idle, Comp Cams offers Thumpr cams in both flat-tappet and hydraulic roller-lifter profiles.

My best advice on camshaft selection is to contact the manufacturer. The intended purpose of the vehicle, vehicle weight, transmission,

Many camshaft options are available for the Mopar big-block, and no other single engine component so dramatically influences the performance characteristics of your engine. Remember that the cam must work with the other components that you incorporate in your engine rebuild. You need to determine the application, ideal torque curve, and horsepower target of your engine in order to make the best choice. Information like intended RPM usage, carburetor size, vehicle weight, transmission type, and rear gear is necessary for determining the correct camshaft for your application. The manufacturer will want to know if you are running a stock or aftermarket intake manifold, exhaust manifolds or headers, and a stock or aftermarket torque converter with higher stall speed.

As mentioned earlier, lifters are available in solid, hydraulic, mechanical roller, and hydraulic roller types. The most aggressive race camshaft that is run today is likely the mechanical roller cam because the mechanical roller lifter (shown) allows for very aggressive profiles. Years of development and testing has brought about excellent reliability and power as a result of using roller cams.

Hydraulic roller lifters in many modern performance cars provide exceptional performance, reliability, and efficiency. The hydraulic roller cam reduces friction that frees up the entire valvetrain, which can translate to better gas mileage. If money is no object, and a high-performance street machine is your goal, a hydraulic roller-lifter camshaft might be your best choice.

Because NHRA requires OEM-style lifters, a hydraulic lifter is mandated for our 1966 383/325-horse engine. However, innovative racers have come up with a hydraulic lifter that works like a solid lifter. NHRA techs are only concerned that if they squeeze the lifter, engine oil comes out of it. Many racers know about Schubeck Lifters, the first company with this design. Smith Machine has taken over the task of making these specialty lifters for racers, and they are better than ever.

The lifter face features a ceramic puck that eliminates the need for cam break in. While on the subject of lifters, remember the advantage that Mopar has in that department with its OEM-size .904-diameter lifters for greater valvetrain stability.

torque converter, rear gear, desired results, and reliability requirements are critical considerations when making a decision as to which camshaft to use. Further, conservative or more radical manners on the street can either make or break an engine build for a particular owner. More than any other single engine component, the camshaft establishes the performance characteristics of a very expensive investment. Don't try to pick a camshaft without consulting experts who can walk you through the selection process.

OEM Cams

Many bone-stock restorations often take some liberties with camshaft selection in order to get a slight horsepower improvement over stock power levels. Mopar Performance offers a number of cams that are perfect for the restorer wanting stock profiles. Almost any aftermarket camshaft provides added performance

One of the great things about working with a big-block Mopar is the excellent attention that was paid to the valvetrain over the years. The factory rocker shaft assembly with stamped rocker arms is far superior to what others offered at the time. In stock form, the B and RB engines have benefitted from stout rocker arm technology. Even if you plan on running a more aggressive cam, the stock rocker arm assembly is likely up to the task.

But anything can bear improvement, and the addition of roller rockers from rockerarms.com or other vendors can upgrade the factory rocker arm shaft assembly for specialized high-performance applications. When you send your rocker arms, techs replace the stock rocker arm shaft with a heavy-duty chrome-moly unit, and do a beautiful job of installing your rockers with new bushings for excellent fit and motion. Rockerarms.com claims that the rockers are good to 7,200 rpm, and frankly, racers I know have run them higher with no problems.

Other options for rocker arm shaft assemblies include 1.60:1 rockers to further enhance cam lift. But before buying these, check your application. Of course, you need to maintain adequate piston-to-valve clearance. My 383 with its closed chamber heads and flat-top pistons meant special attention had to be given to keep the valves from hitting the heads.

that is still good for street duty. Again, all components must support other upgrades, and for that reason, the guys on the Comp Cams tech line are especially helpful.

High-Performance and Race Cams

Bracket racing is not bound by any rules or requirements by a sanctioning body for camshaft profiles. A smart cam choice provides trouble-free rounds of racing without having to do constant maintenance. In NHRA Stock Eliminator racing, the rules dictate the use of factory lift, so camshaft choices are somewhat simpler.

Rocker Arm Assembly

One of the great things about working with a big-block Mopar is the excellent attention that was paid to the valvetrain over the years.

The factory rocker shaft assembly with stamped rocker arms is far superior to what others were offering at the time. In stock form, the B and RB engines have stout rocker arm technology. Even if you plan on running a more aggressive cam, the stock rocker arm assembly is up to the task. But anything can bear improvement, and the addition of roller rockers will allow added performance and reliability.

If the pushrods in your stock engine are straight, retain the proper length, and show little sign of wear on the tips, they can probably be used again for a stock or mild rebuild. Remember, pushrods take a lot of punishment, and common sense says that a new engine deserves a new set of pushrods. Comp Cams builds excellent 3/8-inch-diameter pushrods made of chrome-moly steel that are up to the task of handling more aggressive cam profiles. If you plan on higher valvespring pressures and higher RPM usage, make sure to use reliable pushrods that fit your application. The cam profile determines pushrod length, and in some cases, you may have to purchase custom pushrods that are built to length, as was done with my 383.

Valvesprings are among the most punished and beat-up components in any engine, and therefore, you need to select the best springs for a particular application. Since it's not worth taking the risk of breaking a spring, you should replace them and all other valvetrain components. Break a valvespring, and you can easily end up taking out the cam, lifter, and pushrod. Using a higher lift camshaft means you must examine spring rate and installed spring height. Most stock valve springs are not up to the task of handling high-lift camshafts at higher RPM.

A valvespring upgrade means purchasing matching locks and retainers. There are different styles of locks and retainers that can provide lighter weight and improved reliability for either high-performance street or dedicated race cars. In addition, new technology from Comp Cams with the Beehive-style springs that features progressive spring rate has made it possible to run lower valvespring pressure while still accommodating higher lifts and duration.

Unless your engine has a brand-new timing chain and gear set, count on replacing them when rebuilding your engine. Standard double-roller chains are available for reasonable prices, and perform the necessary task of keeping the camshaft spinning in proper relationship to the crankshaft. Although I am not aware of any presently offered on the market, do not purchase a timing gear set with anything other than steel teeth. The plastic/nylon gears that were installed in the past have proven themselves to be unreliable.

One of my personal favorite "best bang for the buck" upgrades is the Howards Cams Double Roller Billet Steel Timing set. It is built with nine keyways for adjustability, and clearly marked in 2-degree increments. Lightening holes make for a high-tech look. You'll thank yourself for buying it when you start degreeing your cam.

Vendors such as rockerarms.com (formerly Rocker Arm Specialist) can build a factory rocker arm shaft assembly for specialized high-performance applications. Rockerarms.com replaces your stock rocker arm shaft with a heavy-duty chrome-moly unit and does a beautiful job of installing your rockers with new bushings for excellent fit and motion. The company claims that the rockers are good to 7,200 rpm, and frankly, racers I know have run them higher with no problems. Options for building your rocker arm shaft assemblies can also include 1.60:1 rockers to further enhance cam lift. But before buying the 1.60:1 rockers, check your application and remember the importance of maintaining safe piston-to-valve clearance.

OEM Cast-Iron Intake Manifold

Many people use the existing cast-iron intake manifold for a newly rebuilt engine. Clearly, there are a number of benefits to that strategy. Of course, the person interested in restoring a car to OEM specifications uses the cast-iron intake manifold for originality purposes. The low profile of the factory cast-iron manifolds might be necessary where there is little hood clearance for the typical high-rise aftermarket manifold. The obvious benefit of saving money might be the motivation for sticking with the cast-iron manifold.

There are drawbacks to using your stock cast-iron intake manifold. Most aftermarket manifolds outperform the stock units, as has been proven repeatedly on dyno tests. Further, the added weight of the cast-iron intake manifold over an aluminum unit is detrimental to performance. Carburetion choices are often limited when using an OEM intake manifold, so consider your options.

NHRA Intake Manifold Rules

For my racing application, the factory cast-iron intake manifold must be used. Very stringent rules from NHRA are in place concerning intake manifolds, as stated in the rulebook, "Must retain the unaltered stock manifold, consistent with year and engine horsepower claimed. Grinding, sandblasting, or any other modification to manifold prohibited. Any film coating inside manifold prohibited. Runners and plenum must retain OEM appearance."

Fortunately, a number of factory cast-iron 4-barrel manifolds are permitted for NHRA competition. The original manifold (968 casting) that came on the 1966 383 engine is hopeless for power. However, two other manifolds are available for service, castings 666 and 301. Initial testing included using the 301 intake manifold (Hale is convinced that has inherently better runner design). However, in real world testing, the 666 is almost as good as the 301.

A decision on which intake manifold to use for your engine rebuild depends heavily on the camshaft you are using. The camshaft has already dictated a number of other choices in choosing parts for your engine, including cylinder heads, pistons, valvetrain, and exhaust. Retaining the stock cast-iron intake manifold or swapping to a slightly more efficient aftermarket intake makes sense if you run a relatively stock-spec cam with low lift and low-RPM operating range.

If you run a basically stock cam or a slightly more aggressive cam, you could run a dual-plane intake manifold that is close to stock height and it would work well in the idle to the 5,500-rpm range. An Edelbrock Performer 383 carries those specs and brings a noticeable improvement in performance, but doesn't turn you car into an unruly animal on the street.

Think about hood clearance issues in your vehicle before buying that high-rise intake. Do you want to run a scoop or do you need a flat hood? All these issues play into your decision.

Although there are problems with using the stock intake manifold, a number of you will bolt the stock piece back on your engine. For this build, a 301 casting manifold was used, which is a later piece that flows better, and is an accepted legal manifold for NHRA Stock Eliminator. Unless we are talking about a replacement manifold from Mopar, most aftermarket intake manifolds are aluminum. Edelbrock offers the Performer 383 for street duty, the Performer RPM 383 for street/strip applications, and even a dual-quad manifold for nostalgia engines.

The Carter AFB (Aluminum Four Barrel) carburetor is a 4-barrel unit ranging in size from 500 to 750 cfm. All AFB carburetors have four metering jets, with the primary jets being larger than the secondary jets. Properly set up, the AFB's mechanical secondaries ensure immediate response and maximum performance at wide-open throttle. Dean Oliver, owner of Deano's Carburetors, is rebuilding AFB specifically for NHRA Stock Eliminator racing. Dean is one of the premier carburetor guys in drag racing.

Aftermarket Intake Manifolds

If you opt for a higher-flowing and lighter-weight aluminum intake manifold for the street, select a dual-plane design. It features a smaller plenum than a single-plane carb and a higher air speed at lower RPM, providing a stronger fuel charge at low RPM. Remember, a street engine is driven at much lower RPM than a race engine.

Edelbrock offers its Performer 383 for street duty, the Performer RPM 383 for street/strip applications, and a dual-quad manifold for nostalgia engines. The number of choices for intake manifolds is huge when looking at race applications, and for the most part comes down to preference. Work with your engine builder on induction needs, and ask around when coming up with the best choice for your application.

Airflow velocity is the key to making this relatively small Carter AFB carburetor work efficiently. Ultimately, performance comes back to cylinder seal and the vacuum produced by the optimum piston and ring package. The speed of the air/fuel mixture is dependent on the vacuum created by the intake stroke. That vacuum signals the need for more fuel sent to the main boosters in the carb.

Unlike a street or road racing application, drag racing is primarily interested in the fuel mixture at wide-open throttle. The task of proper fuel-curve calibration is a matter of trial and error for a particular combination. The accelerator pump is critical for controlling throttle response and launch. The accelerator pump can be fine-tuned with various squirters to manage fuel delivery. Additional tweaking can come by way of changing the position of the pump arm.

The Carter AFB flow-sensing secondary air valves monitor wide-open-throttle launches. With the secondaries open, these air valves regulate the air/fuel mixture flow to meet demand and capacity. Properly tuned, bog is eliminated at launch.

If one of the reasons for rebuilding your engine was the problem of constant overheating, it is critical that you examine the external components of the cooling system before concluding that the overheating was an engine problem.

In other words, is the radiator working properly? Were the belts properly adjusted? Was the coolant level full? Was the fan working properly, and is the fan shroud intact? Since the oil absorbs heat from the engine, is the oil level full?

Overheating can occur if there is a blown head gasket, a stuck thermostat, clogged water passages in the engine, or coolant leaks. As the engine is being torn down, attempt to determine why your engine was overheating. Warped and cracked heads, bearing failure, and oil starvation can all contribute.

When rebuilding your engine, make sure to consider which radiator, thermostat, heater core, and water pump you want. If you are restoring your car to stock specs, the OEM water pump is sufficient. If you are building a high-performance street car, an aftermarket electric water pump like the one built by Meziere is a good choice. Not only is parasitic drag diminished, but cooling efficiency is improved.

Mechanical Water Pumps

The cost of a replacement water pump for a big-block Mopar is less than $50, so this is a good time to replace it. However, keep your old one if you do. If you ever sell the car, some collectors appreciate seeing every part that came with the car, even if it is worn out and not salvageable.

*With ARP's full selection of high-quality fasteners available for just about every applica-*tion, the days of reusing bolts are over. Even if you are doing a stock rebuild, about an extra $200 gets you just about every bolt needed. Especially critical in any rebuild is replacing connecting rod bolts, and ARP has you covered with its patented Wave-Loc technology. The use of ARP main cap bolts allowes you to torque main caps to 100 ft-lbs, as opposed to only 85 ft-lbs for the stock main cap bolts.

ARP Part Description	Part Number
Pro Wave ARP2000 Connecting Rod Bolts	245-6402
Head Bolts, Pro Series	245-3706
Damper Bolt Kit	240-2501
Engine and Accessory Fastener Kit, Black Oxide 12 Point	545-9701
Flexplate Bolt Kit, Pro Series	200-2905
Cam Bolt Kit	244-1001
Main Bolts	140-5001

Thermostat

The thermostat blocks the flow of coolant from the engine, allowing the engine to warm up more quickly. Once the engine reaches desired operating temperature, the thermostat opens and allows normal coolant flow. The typical operating temperature for street-driven vehicles is about 180 to 195 degrees F.

To test a thermostat, boil a pan of water with a thermometer in the water, hold the thermostat with tongs, and lower it into the boiling water at its rated opening temperature. If the thermostat opens properly that means it is operating correctly. Observe whether the thermostat closes after it is removed from the hot water. A stuck thermostat causes the car's engine to overheat, so spending a few bucks for a new thermostat at rebuild time is money well spent.

Thermostat housings are prone to cracking. When a thermostat is replaced, it is very easy to over tighten the bolts to the housing. Inspect the thermostat housing carefully for cracks, especially if you have any coolant at the base of the thermostat housing.

Headers

Street cars perform better after you make the swap from the restrictive factory exhaust manifolds to the free-flowing headers. Though the temptation might be to pick up a used set of headers if money is tight, be forewarned that headers, especially those that are not coated properly, can be subject to corrosion from the intense heat of the exhaust gases.

Hooker Super Comp headers offer 1-inch primary tubes and ceramic coating. There is no question that the benefits for freeing up exhaust flow are absolutely essential for any kind of performance application.

Fasteners

Dollar for dollar, buying new bolts and fasteners from ARP is money well spent. With ARP's full selection of high-quality fasteners available for just about every application, the days of reusing bolts are over. Even if you are doing a stock rebuild, about an extra $200 gets you just about every bolt needed. Especially critical in any rebuild is replacing connecting rod bolts, and ARP has you covered with its patented Wave-Loc technology. The use of ARP main cap bolts allowed us to torque the main caps to 100 ft-lbs, as opposed to only 85 ft-lbs for the stock main cap bolts.

Although appearance of the completed engine is secondary to its performance, the goal is to give our 383 stocker engine an industrial, all-business look. For that reason, the nod went to the black-oxide-finish 8740 chrome-moly bolts. ARP's Engine & Accessory Fastener Kit includes the bolts for installing the intake manifold, thermostat, water pump, oil pan, coil bracket, distributor bracket, front cover, valve covers, headers, engine mounts, fuel pump, and alternator bracket.

MACHINE WORK AND SHORT BLOCK BUILD-UP

After disassembly, the engine is merely a pile of parts. Many parts cannot be reconditioned or reused, but a number of them are in need of machine work. This chapter details machine shop work to be performed on your engine components. Although this isn't work you can do at home by yourself, you do need to have a thorough understanding of it so you can adeptly guide your engine through the process. After all, your goal is to have your rebuilt engine perform reliably and at its horsepower target.

To get a reasonable look at the condition of the cylinder walls, quickly shoot the walls with some WD-40, and use the stone wheel to remove any built-up corrosion or residue. This cleanup step provides a marked improvement in the appearance of the block, and makes further inspection much easier. Break out the dial indicator and measure the cylinder bores. (Measuring this block shows it to be standard bore, and believed to be untouched.) Apply solvent to the outside of the block, and scrape off any residual grease or grime. This block had two pistons frozen to the cylinder walls, but after an initial cleanup, it was determined that the cylinder walls had only minor pock marks that would easily clean up with a .060-inch overbore.

Clean and Debur the Heads

If your engine is dirty and grimy, clean it up prior to getting it Magnafluxed and bored.

Initial Cleaning

Using plenty of solvent, take a ball brush to the cylinders in order to get a better look at what you have. Scrape away any gasket residue, and use a wire brush to get rid of oily grime. If you have access to a hot tank, use it—maybe more than once. Stubborn grime might call for some creative measures, including a wire brush drill attachment, an acetylene torch to attack baked on grime, and scrapers of various shapes and sizes.

Choose a Cylinder Block

In a ground-up restoration of a muscle car, it is extremely important that the car be restored with its original drivetrain. For example, attempting to rebuild a numbers-matching engine with a damaged block can be a catastrophe. Casting numbers and build-date stampings can often increase the value of a muscle car by 25 to even 100 percent, depending on the particular car.

Some engine blocks can be rebuilt with a simple overbore. However, through use and time, many blocks do not clean up even with a .060-inch overbore. Some blocks have cracks in high-stress areas, such as the main bearing saddles. Other blocks have already gone through one or two previous rebuilds and do not have enough cylinder material left and cannot be overbored. It could be that it makes no sense to work with the original block, or the repair to make the block usable is cost prohibitive. Repairs to cast iron can be accomplished, but it is a specialized art form, and is expensive.

The choice is yours: you can store the original engine and find a good replacement block or you can build a sound, strong, virgin block. I know of a particular high-dollar 409 Chevy Bel Air that continually brings home car show awards with a date-correct, highly detailed engine, while the original engine is safely stored in the owner's garage. Any question as to the originality of the engine is answered by the status of the original engine being in the possession of the owner. Most potential customers are satisfied knowing that it exists. Even though damaged, as long as the original engine is included in the purchase, the value is usually only slightly affected.

The selection of a block is extremely critical because if the block is flawed the engine fails. If a high-performance engine fails at the track, safety becomes an issue. Emotional attachment to engine components is not the way to build a safe, reliable engine. Building your 440 engine that came out of your dad's 1972 Chrysler New Yorker with 300,000 miles might make for a cool story but it wouldn't be worth it if it needed three sleeves in order to bring it up to buildable standards.

Because of the critical nature of the block as the foundation of the rest of the engine, thoroughly inspect it before you buy it. Measure the main bearing saddles, measure the cylinder bores, check for any repairs, and do not hesitate to discard a block that "looked good." Do not just believe what you are told about your engine. Check, measure, test, and measure again.

Deburring

Using proper eye protection, deburring starts with a hammer and chisel. As an aside, certain parts of the cylinder heads also need to be deburred, so whether you are working on the block or the heads, be very careful to have an awareness of working in areas that could be damaged by a hit from the hammer, or prolonged exposure to the grinding wheel. Remember, you are working around water jackets and ports that might be thin in some areas. Although the temptation might be to make the block look perfectly smooth, that extra grinding might lead to a disaster.

Use straight and tapered cartridge rolls in both 40- and 80-grit to create a less restrictive and smoother surface for oil flow. A shortage of oil in the pan can lead to oil starvation, while too much oil in the top end of the engine produces oil leaks and oil ingestion through the intake side of the cylinder head. These conditions can be disastrous to any rebuilt engine, especially high-performance and race engines that see higher RPM usage. Both the oil return holes in the valley between the cylinder banks and the surfaces of the cylinder bank walls that make up the sides of the valley must be smooth.

The main bearing webs need to be deburred. Light deburring can be performed on the sharp edges and corners of the main bearing caps and oil pump mating surface. A number of sharp edges along the lifter bores and exterior surfaces of the block must also be addressed.

During the 383 rebuild, casting flash was discovered in the intake and exhaust ports of the head. For most rebuilds, creative angling of the grinder reaches most problem areas. Since NHRA rules for Stock Eliminator prohibit any grinding in the ports, a hammer and chisel were used to break off the offending residue.

During the deburring process, make sure to smooth the edges along the pan rail. Take the time to carefully chamfer the oil drain holes in the lifter valley, but don't make the lifter valley area perfectly smooth. The as-cast bumpy surface in the lifter valley aids heat transfer from the block to the oil. From the casting process, the block has a significant amount of casting slag that affects oil circulation and flow and could cause it to break off during operation causing severe damage to the engine. While grinding, watch for any cracks or abnormalities in the casting.

Deburring the block is the process of grinding off all the burrs and casting slag remaining from production. Deburring the block also calls for grinding down many of the sharp edges on the block. The process is necessary for a number of reasons. By deburring certain areas, it helps prevent stress-induced cracking and failures. In addition, if you remove the main bearing web-casting flash, the block can withstand more horsepower and better resist stress cracking. Most importantly, many of the places that are ground down have the potential to lead to cracks. Functionally, deburring ensures that all the oiling passages in the block are clear. Further, a smoother surface on areas like the lifter valley speeds oil return to the pan. Also, the block becomes easier and safer to handle, essentially minimizing the chance of getting cut and nicked as you handle it during the build. Depending on how dedicated you are to the process, deburring makes the block look better and removes some weight in the process.

You can use a simple grinding tool to carefully grind down seams left from the mold. Though this step is relatively simple, take care to avoid contact with areas like the main bearing saddles, cylinder walls, and lifter bores. Though somewhat tedious, this process should only be handled while the block is bare, so be thorough and complete. Deburring the block not only aids oil flow and return, it also ensures that pieces of slag and casting flash do not break loose and damage internal engine components.

Once the deburring is completed, a thorough cleaning is absolutely essential in order to remove any trace of flash, machining debris, and cutting oil used during machining. Inspect all threaded holes, oil passages, and coolant passages. Use hot, soapy water and solvent, followed by a cleaning of cylinder bores with brushes and compressed air.

Select a Good Shop

Few enthusiasts have a completely equipped machine shop in their garage. You are therefore at the mercy of a machinist who has the equipment. There are many good craftsmen out there who know how to perform these necessary procedures.

Making use of all the resources available to you, determine the type of machine shop you require and begin your hunt. Understand that not every place is the same, and some have a certain specialty with particular brands and applications. Choose a shop that has good track record for rebuilding Mopar big-blocks.

One way to create a list of possible shops available for the build is to ask around for recommendations. You might be surprised how many friends, family members, and acquaintances have a tip for you.

Internet forums are a particular help in this area, such as the Mopar Only forum. I've always had my questions answered quickly on the forum. Register on an active forum of your choice and post a thread asking for recommendations for quality machine shops in your area. Make sure to thank those who post helpful information, as it greatly aids continued assistance when questions arise.

You can get further help in finding a quality machine shop at local car shows, cruise nights, and racing venues. Car people are happy to give details concerning their car build, especially engine details.

Narrow the field to two or three shops, and don't settle on a shop until you receive at least three strong recommendations for it. Good shops are not hard to find, but bad shops with poor-quality results and long

66 HOW TO REBUILD THE BIG-BLOCK MOPAR

turn-around times do somehow manage to stay in business.

Take the time to call the shop prior to a final decision. Spend time talking to the owner to get a feel for his willingness to answer questions. You have a lot of interaction with the machinist during a project, so make sure communication is comfortable and effective. Ask him about his equipment. Schedule a tour of the shop to get a feel for its cleanliness and professionalism. An unwillingness to comply to some simple requests prior to the build often spells trouble for the future. Though a local high-quality shop is ideal, don't rule out driving a few miles to gain the advantages of a skilled builder.

Finally, compare pricing. Most machine shops have a standard price list of services, either online or in printed form. Get prices before you commit, and compare! Quality work might involve higher costs for the same service, so ask the engine builder to explain differences between his price and other shops. Many engine shops do not take the time to finish cylinders properly, and though their pricing might be less than another high-quality shop, you definitely get what you pay for.

Machine Shop Procedures

For cylinder preparation, cylinders must be bored with a boring bar that is either deck mounted or located by the crank. When boring, at least .003 to .005 inch should be left for the final hone. In other words, if the cylinder is receiving a .060 overbore, the boring machine performs a .055 overbore, and .005 is accomplished by the final honing machine

The final finish of the cylinder walls should be as suggested by the piston ring manufacturer. Other procedures must be accomplished correctly by your machinist, including cylinder deck preparation, rod reconditioning, crank preparation, and cylinder head preparation.

Align Honing and Align Boring

Looking at an engine block might lead the casual observer to conclude that it is rigid, and could never change shape in any way. However, the original casting process at the factory can distort a block, leaving residual stress in the new casting. Over time, expansion and contraction from heating and cooling causes significant warpage. If the engine has seen higher stress and heat because of a racing or heavy-duty application, warpage can be significant, leading to premature failure.

Improper maintenance of the engine during its life is another reason for out-of-round main bearing bores or camshaft bores. This is often a result of failure to perform standard maintenance such as to the cooling system, oil changes, and fuel system upkeep. High miles on even a well-maintained engine could eventually necessitate a complete rebuild that includes align boring the main bearing and camshaft bores.

Although Mopar guys might tend to think that Mopar makes the best parts, incorrect bore center alignment can come from the factory. In a perfect world, the camshaft bore and crankshaft bore should be parallel in the block. However, we do not live in a perfect world. Align boring the crankshaft and camshaft bores corrects any misalignment in the block, be it from less-than-ideal manufacturing tolerances, or improper assembly leading to premature failure. If an engine receives new alumi-num or steel main caps, align honing becomes an absolute necessity.

For engines under the 600-hp ceiling, the opinion of most engine builders is that the OEM iron two-bolt main caps in the B and RB Mopar big-blocks are more than adequate for keeping the bottom end together, even for 7,000-plus-rpm blasts. This engine features two-bolt main caps using ARP main cap bolts. The use of ARP bolts over the stock main cap bolts moves the installation torque spec from 85 to 100 ft-lbs.

Whether the goal is peace of mind or future power upgrades, some owners upgrade their engine's bottom end with two-bolt aluminum main caps. They believe this allows the crank to flex slightly without suffering breakage. Others say that the differing expansion rates of the aluminum caps and cast-iron block cause problems. Many engine builders have successfully used the aluminum caps and they appear to be a good option for OEM production blocks, especially when used with proper ARP main bolts.

Options exist to convert the big-block Mopar from a two-bolt main to four-bolt mains using an aftermarket cross-bolted main conversion. However, that conversion calls for precise drilling into the pan rail of the block. Drilling holes into the pan rail of a two-bolt main block, in my opinion, only introduces six new places for the block to crack. If you're doing a high-performance rebuild and the target is 600 or more horsepower, you need a four-bolt main block. As mentioned in Chapter 5, you can purchase a Keith Black, World Products, or Koleno Performance block that is cast with provisions for cross-bolted mains.

As a precaution, an undersized tap is used to clean the threads so as to

Align Honing and Align Boring

Of all the steps in preparing a block for rebuilding, the crankshaft centerline is the most critical. All major machining processes for the block are based on the crank centerline, and if it is not true, the block is not square. The camshaft bearing bores must be square to the main bearing bores, or there will be premature bearing wear, bearing failure, and catastrophic damage to the engine itself.

2 Decking the Block with the BHJ Fixture

After the align honing is completed, the next step is to deck the block. (The block deck height for a B is 9.98 inches; for an RB, it is 10.725.) The deck of a V-8 engine block is the top portion of the cylinder bore that serves as the mating surface of the cylinder heads. Decking is the need for the block to be cut and leveled in order to create a perfectly flat mating surface for the cylinder heads. If the block is not decked, head gasket failure, coolant leaks, or compression loss can result.

Working from the crankshaft centerline, the deck surfaces must be perfectly square to the block. In order to mount the block on the decking machine, this BHJ fixture and support bar is mounted to the block with collar and end caps. The block is now ready to be hoisted to the decking machine.

1 Hone the Cap

One of the key factors in line boring is to make sure that most of the honing occurs on the cap, and not on the main bearing saddles of the block. That is critical in maintaining the proper distance between the crankshaft and the camshaft. If the honing depends on cutting the main bearing saddles, the timing chain is not as tight as necessary.

Measurements are taken at various points in the bore to guarantee that a perfect circle is being created. A dial indicator measures the bore, and then is moved about 90 degrees in the bore for a second reading, which eventually is the same as the first as the machine recreates the original-spec bore. Every main bore is examined carefully, with the goal of making the main bore perfectly round by taking the metal out of the main cap. The honing mandrel passes through the main bores for a short time until the operator at Van Senus Machine Shop stops and measures the main bearing bore with a dial indicator.

Care is taken to stop and let the main bores cool down during honing. Too much heat leads to expansion and an inaccurate reading.

When the block returns from Jim Lewis Race Engines, the main bearing bore is checked with a dial bore gauge, and measures exactly to specification. The line bore is confirmed to be correct. As each main cap is reinstalled, it is torqued to spec.

3 Level the Block

The block must be mounted perfectly level so that all milling angles are square. Finer adjustments are made to get the block exactly in place.

4 Measure the Block

The block is measured using a micrometer to determine that it is parallel to the cutting stones on the decking machine.

5 Resurface the Deck

The goal is to produce a perfectly level mating surface for the heads and the intake manifold. The block is resurfaced to bring it to zero deck height. The plate centers the block with the line-honed main bore and cam bore to produce a perfect 90-degree angle. The decking machine passes over the block, and removes a couple thousandths from the deck on each pass. The job is done when the entire block has a clean cut surface. This block is set up to allow the deck to be surfaced.

6 Clean Cut the Main Cap

A Sunnen grinder is used to take a few thousandths off the main caps. By doing so the main bearing bore is reduced, and must be opened up again. Really good operators take the meat out of the cap, and not out of the block, in order to restore a perfectly round bore to spec. If the operator corrects the roundness of the hole by taking material out of the block, the center-to-center distance of the timing gears slightly decreases. As a result, the timing chain tension slightly loosens and that has to be corrected. At this time a machinist takes a fine file and cleans the main cap parting lines on the block saddles to be sure the mating surface is clean.

produce accurate torque wrench readings. After the main caps have been ground true on the Sunnen grinding machine, they are installed in the block (without any bearings of course) and tightened to recommended specifications. The cylinder block is dialed-in and positioned for line boring. The honing mandrel is moved in and out by the operator while lubricating oil is pumped onto the honing stones.

Boring the Block

At this point, the block has been cleaned, hot tanked, deburred, align honed, and decked. The bare cylinder block is now "square" and ready to be bored in preparation for new rings and possibly new pistons, depending on the extent of your build. By

boring the cylinders, any deep scoring, scratches, and irregularities in the roundness of the cylinder are removed from the block.

Typical overbore sizes are .020, .030, .040, and .060 inch. The question becomes: How big should I bore the cylinders? They should be bored only as much as needed to clean up the cylinder walls, unless you want to get every cubic inch of displacement out of the engine as possible.

A few factors come into play here. A sonic tester determines how much iron is available in the block, and whether there is enough for your desired overbore. The area of metal thickness is also important. A cylinder needs to be thicker on the top where combustion heat is the most

intense and stress on the cylinder is greatest. A cylinder that's thinner on the bottom but within specs is acceptable because this area of the cylinder is subjected to less heat and the main webbing provides more support than the top of the cylinder. A sonic tester is especially helpful if you are choosing between a number of blocks for your rebuild.

For many years, information circulated about the final years of the B/RB blocks being "thin wall" castings and not desirable for rebuilding. Various year ranges were quoted via engine manuals and various magazine articles. Though 1978 was the last year the engines were produced, some reported that the blocks made from 1973 to 1978 were thin-wall

The operator chooses the overbore size, such as on this Winona Van Norman boring machine. By enlarging the cylinders, not only is displacement added, but the resulting cylinder wall is made perfectly round and consistent throughout the entire travel of the piston against the cylinder walls. Of course, overboring an engine requires new pistons to fit the larger cylinder walls. The machine shop should use a torque plate when overboring the cylinders. This ensures that bores are optimally aligned and ultimately the cylinders provide the best ring seal. Typical overbore sizes are .020, .030, .040, .060, and .070 inch.

castings, while others put the years of thin-wall castings from 1976 to 1978. It was circulated that these thin-wall castings should not be overbored more than .020 or .030 at the most.

Fortunately, 440Source, Inc., a key supplier of big-block Mopar stroker kits and engine components for the B/RB engines, investigated the claims to see if there were "thin wall" B/RB castings in the later years of production. It sonic tested more than 50 blocks and debunked that myth. Its findings were that the 1973 to 1978 blocks did not have thinner cylinder walls, and that many of those blocks

had thicker metal around the main bearing saddles, and were in some ways, the best B/RB blocks made.

The conclusion 440Source came to was that the very best block Chrysler ever made was the 1972 to 1973 400 B Block, which had the most metal in that critical main bearing saddle. However, automotive journalist and author Andy Finkbeiner reported he performed hardness testing of the later blocks, and found that the strength of the iron of the blocks made from 1976 to 1978 was reduced about 10 percent as measured on the Brinell hardness scale. Apparently, material strength decreased for the last three years of production.

Final Hone

An overboring machine typically stops about .005 inch from the total desired overbore dimension in order to leave room for the final honing procedure. The final hone

Final Hone Process

An overboring machine typically leaves .005 inch of the total amount of overbore desired in order to allow for the final honing procedure. In other words, a .060 total overbore is accomplished by performing a .055 cut with the cylinder boring machine, and a .005 cut from the finish honing machine.

An overbore of about .060 is about all you want on a B/RB Chrysler engine. When performing the honing process, head gaskets are put on the block to replicate the stress that the block will experience. Spend the extra money to reserve one set of head gaskets for the honing process and another set for final assembly.

The plates are torqued down as are the cylinder heads in order to create the exact conditions under which the block will be stressed. The honing stones are inserted and various grits are used to produce a final, glass-like finish. (Lewis started with 280-grit stones, then 320-grit, then 400-grit, and then completed the process with a honing brush.) An operator may stand at the honing machine for hours moving the honing arm up and down until the particular stones have finished their work. A faster movement produces larger angles of cuts in the final hone, while a slower movement reduces that angle.

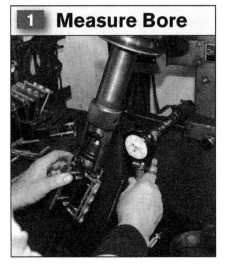

1 Measure Bore

The dial bore indicator is inserted into the cylinders to check the progress. Standard bore for a 383 engine is 4.250 inches. Figuring the overbore of .060, the final cylinder bore is 4.310.

2 Final Hone Operation

As the honing stones are moved up and down they create the desired cross-hatch pattern of very fine scratches that serve as places where the oil can remain on the cylinder walls, providing lubrication to the piston rings. Honing fluid both lubricates the cutting stones and washes the metal particles coming off the cylinder walls.

3 Chamfer the Bore

To give the piston rings the ability to enter the cylinder, the top edge of the cylinder must be slightly chamfered. One way is to simply take a piece of 180-grit emery cloth and carefully sand the top edge.

4 Chamfer the Oil Feed Holes

The oil feed holes that come down through the main bearing saddles are chamfered. A wire and cleaning brush is used to make sure each hole is free from obstruction.

5 Chase Threads in Block

Cleaning all the threaded holes is a big part of engine block preparation. First the thread is cleaned with solvent and a brush, and then shot with compressed air. A thread chaser is used to clean the threads, and again cleaned with solvent. If the chaser is the proper size for the hole, plenty of WD-40 is used. If the threads are not clean the bolts don't hold the accurate torque spec. And certainly, an engine fastener that is over- or undertorqued can lead to fastener failure and then outright engine failure.

provides the proper cylinder wall finish to create optimal ring seal and lubrication. The final hone essentially smoothes the rough surface that is left from the boring machine. Various grades of abrasive stones are used in the honing process to leave a surface that is optimal for the piston ring package.

Connecting Rods Prep

One of the major decisions you have to make is which connecting rod to use. The various OEM pistons and pressed piston pins and connecting rods were more than adequate for street duty. In fact, even many race cars successfully campaigned their cars with stock connecting rods with no complaints about the rods. The most common rod failure is related to either a spun bearing or broken rod bolt.

Most street cars do fine with stock connecting rods. Prices are relatively reasonable for new connecting rods and can be a good investment for that added measure of protection for

The machinist takes particular care when washing the crankshaft. It must not be knocked over or rolled around during cleaning because it could bend. He scrubs the crank with solvent and then pressure washes it. He cleans the exterior of the crank with a soft brush so he doesn't scratch or damage the journals or machined surfaces. Now is a great time to take a closer look at all the journals, and the machinist keeps an eye out for scratches, gouges, and other imperfections. He inspects the crank key, flange, and threads in the crank to make sure they are not stripped or damaged. He uses small-diameter brushes to clean the bolt holes and the oil passages.

Crankshaft Considerations

Big-block B/RB Mopar engines offer some great possibilities for swapping parts. At the same time, there are differences between the B and RB engines. The biggest difference between the two is the crankshaft main bearing journal diameters. B engines (361, 383, 400) feature a 2.625 main bearing journal diameter, while the RB engine crankshafts come equipped with a 2.750 main bearing journal diameter. Both cranks share a 2.375-inch connecting rod journal diameter.

The 383-ci engine was nicely equipped with a forged crank until 1971 when it was decided to put a cast-iron crank in a 383 2-barrel engine. The 383 cast-crank engine had to be externally balanced and came with its own unique vibration dampener and torque converter. Put simply, avoid using the cast crank from the 383 engine. Forged cranks from the earlier engines are still available and eliminate the need for external balancing. A later block that came with a cast crank and external balancing can easily be converted to a forged steel crank.

After the block, crank, rods, and heads have been magnafluxed, it is time to begin the machining operations. A competent machine shop must regrind the crankshaft. In a 7,200-rpm-potential 383 race engine, the crankshaft must run absolutely straight. The crank is then ground .010 inch undersized on the main journals, and .020 under on the rod journals. When the rod journals are underground, they are also indexed, and the stroke is equalized. Essentially, the journals are cut to ensure that the connecting rod throws are exactly 90 degrees apart.

the piston. If you decide to use the pressed-fit pin, the machine shop needs to press the pin into the small end of the rod, through the piston.

The block, crankshaft, and rods must be Magnafluxed, paying special attention to areas that are prone to cracking. The high-stress areas are critical and you must carefully examine them at this time.

Built into the design of all Wedge cranks is an undercut fillet, which is not as strong as a full-radius crank. Check the crank journals with the crankshaft out of the block. Measure the diameter of the main bearing journals and the connecting rod journals. They should be within .0005 of the factory specifications.

Next, place the crank back in the block supported by the number-1 and number-5 caps and bearings. Position a dial indicator against the center main bearing journal and rotate the crank to see if there is any variance in the measurement. Ideally, you want .0000 runout, but .002 is acceptable; .004 is the most runout you want in your crank.

Excessive runout, out-of-round condition, or irregularities on the journals call for having the crank reground. Call it engine builder eti-

Once the crank has been cleaned with solvent and dried with compressed air, it is imperative that both the main and rod journals are measured with a micrometer. Even though this crank is an uncut, virgin piece in good condition, it is determined that the main journals need to be ground .010 undersize, and the rod journals, .020 under. If the crank journals have deeper scratches, gouges, or other imperfections, the crank would require either a .020 or .030 cut to remove the flaws.

your rotating assembly. If there is a possibility of reusing your existing rods, they must be checked. Measure the bearing bores to see if they have become enlarged or out of round.

When building an engine, the small end of the rod must be prepped for the piston pin. There are two kinds of piston pins—pressed and floating. A pressed-fit pin is the OEM method of attaching the rod to

quette, but don't take your crank to have it ground without doing your very best job to clean it. If you have access to a machine shop, hot tank the crank at least a couple of times, using solvent between washings to remove as much grime as possible.

Big-Block Mopar Crankshafts		
Part Number	Engine	Material
2268114	383 4-barrel	Forged
3462922	383/400 2-barrel	Cast, externally balanced
3672000	400 4-barrel	Cast crank
2536983	1967–1971 440 4-barrel	Forged
3512036	1970–1972 440 6-barrel	Forged, externally balanced
3671283	1972–1973 440 4-barrel	Forged
3671242	1973 440 4-barrel	Forged, balanced for different weight pistons
3751889	1974 440 2- & 4-barrel	Cast, externally balanced
3751899	1974 440	Forged
2406240	413/426 Max Wedge	Forged (ultimate factory RB crankshaft)

Main Bearing Journal Diameters

Engine	Inches
361, 383, 400	2.625
440	2.750

Connecting Rod Journal Diameters

Engine	Inches
361, 383, 400, 440	2.375

Now that the block is clean, check it, the crank, and the connecting rods for cracks. If the block was subjected to freezing, overheating, or extreme stress from high-RPM usage, cracks may have occurred in critical areas that make your block unsuitable for a rebuild. Those critical areas include the block's main webbing, which supports the crankshaft saddles, the sides of the block, and the cylinder walls. Remember that it's possible the block was defective from the factory, resulting in thin spots in the block—just because a block looks good does not ensure that it is flawless. Dumping money into a block that is cracked is a waste, in which case a replacement block should be located.

The Magnaflux process involves using a Magnaflux instrument to create a strong magnetic field on the engine block. A colored iron powder is sprinkled in the area of the magnetic field, and if a crack is present, it collects in the crack, producing a prominent line. Though some larger cracks might be visible to the naked eye, many situations exist where a block is cracked and can only be revealed by the Magnaflux machine. The careful machinist inspects all components, and recommends a replacement part when a crack shows up during inspection.

With the crank close to where it needs to be for balancing, the journals are polished. Here, Jim holds a motor-driven sanding belt with 400-grit emery paper while Everett slowly spins the crank. Jim moves the paper over the bearing journals in order to polish out any minor scratches or nicks until it has a highly polished, mirror finish.

With the machining operations completed, the crank is thoroughly cleaned with solvent. Brushes are used to completely clean all oil holes and crevices on the crank. After the crank has been completely cleaned with solvent, it is squirted with engine oil, making sure to get oil in all the holes, especially the oil hole so that it is protected. Then the crank is set aside to await assembly.

MOCKING UP HEADS AND VALVETRAIN

Second only to camshaft selection, cylinder head choice largely determines the characteristics of your engine's performance and impacts most other decisions on how to build your B/RB engine. Slapping random parts together without any thought to how each one contributes to the engine's overall performance results in a poor-running final product. You must carefully select compatible parts for the heads and valvetrain. These pieces work as an integrated system, so cams, valves, lifters, pushrods, rockers, and related parts must work in harmony.

If you're performing a strict stock rebuild, use only stock parts. If you're building a slightly modified or high-performance engine, you need to select aftermarket parts that are compatible. If you're building a slightly stronger street engine, the cam needs to suit the valve lift, rocker geometry, adequate valvespring pressure, and so forth. Engine components must be correctly matched to deliver an engine's full potential. That philosophy is especially critical when making the final decision on cylinder heads.

Cylinder Heads

I discuss some cylinder head options in Chapter 5. Now let's look at making the choice between OEM

If you are working with cylinder heads that were on your engine, and the engine checked out well with a compression test, or a leak-down test, you can have some measure of confidence that the heads have a good likelihood of being nice candidates for rebuild. If you are purchasing a used head, be ready for the dreaded consequence that there could be a crack in the head that would render it unusable.

A test that reveals the condition of the valve seats is to pour a solvent in the combustion chambers and allow the head to sit overnight. If the solvent leaks into the ports, you need to resurface the valves and the valve seats. The head must be disassembled, cleaned, visually inspected, and then Magnafluxed. The rocker arm shaft assembly is the first component to remove from the head. Use a 9/16-inch socket wrench to loosen the bolts. Be careful to hold onto the retainers underneath the bolts, and mark the bolts for future use, as they are not all the same size.

and aftermarket heads. Purchasing entry-level aftermarket heads costs about the same as performing a basic valve job and replacing valveguides and seats on your original-equipment heads. New valves, modifications for oversize valves, new valvesprings and hardware, plus any porting and polishing work drive the price of your rebuilt heads even higher, making the choice between OEM and aftermarket heads even more difficult. In the end, a rebuilt set of heads could easily be more expensive than a new set of aftermarket units.

The deciding factor again becomes application. If you're restoring a numbers-matching collector

car, a basic rebuild of the OEM heads is preferred, so as to preserve the originality of the car. Other motivations for avoiding the purchase of aftermarket heads could include either the desire to make the original equipment fast or the necessity to work with OEM heads because of the rules of a sanctioning body, like NHRA. If you want to build a high-performance street car or street/strip car, aftermarket heads are a far better option than stock heads for increasing flow and therefore performance.

Strict adherence to the NHRA rulebook drives the building of this engine, which requires OEM heads, for my 1966 Coronet. For that reason, 45-year-old OEM cylinder heads must be rebuilt to perform at optimal levels. Most of the work on these cylinder heads is directly applicable to rebuilding a set of OEM heads for

the 1967 Chrylser Newport, but tips for maximum flow and breathing are also discussed.

This head is one of a pair that I purchased for $300 in untouched condition. The ports have not been gasket matched, the chambers are unmolested, and vavletrain hardware looks original. These are 915 casting heads with the smaller, 1.60-inch exhaust valve. After the cylinder heads were visually checked for cracks and overall condition, they were disassembled, cleaned, and Magnafluxed. If you have the funds, it is best to have a couple pairs of heads on hand, in order to choose the best pair. Also it's good to have two sets in case a head is not usable.

These 1967 915 casting heads are great examples of closed-chamber heads. The combustion chambers are only large enough to make room for

Big-block Mopar cylinder heads came with either open- or closed-combustion chamber designs. The 1968-and-newer cylinder heads were the open-chamber design. Open-chamber heads are built with round combustion chambers that match the shape of the cylinder bore. They are far more common than 1967-and-earlier big-block Mopar heads with a closed-chamber design. The 1963-and-older B/RB engines used four-bolt valve covers, while the 1964-and-newer engines used a six-bolt configuration for the valve covers. With the exception of Max Wedge heads, which require a specific intake manifold, all B/RB heads interchange. However, closed-chamber heads on an open-chamber short block will probably result in the piston hitting the head.

These 1967 915 casting heads are great examples of closed-chamber heads. Each combustion chamber is equipped with a 2.08-inch intake valve, a 1.60 exhaust valve, and a spark plug hole. This design, in theory, aids flow. In the 383 engine, the closed-chamber heads incorporate a flat-top piston, without any kind of dome or valve relief. This configuration makes it a bit tricky to increase cam lift because the valve hits the piston. For that reason, piston-to-valve clearance must be carefully checked while assembling an engine with these heads. (See Chapter 9 for information on taking this measurement.)

A pneumatic valvespring compressor is designed in a C-clamp fashion, where the top of the compressor is placed over the valvesprings, which then cups the spring and retainer. The bottom portion of the tool wraps around the cylinder head and is positioned over the valve face to hold the valve in place. When all is properly positioned, air compresses the plunger-type mechanism to compress the spring, allowing the operator to remove the locks and retainer. If the spring is stuck, it receives a tap from a ballpeen hammer, which loosens the spring retainer and keepers.

the 2.08-inch intake valve, the 1.60 exhaust valve, and the spark plug hole. This design, in theory, aided flow. Open-chambers are built with combustion chambers with the same diameter as the cylinder bore.

Valve Jobs

A "valve job" on a street car involves removing the cylinder heads from the engine. To disassemble the heads, the rocker arm assembly, valvesprings with their retainers and keepers, and valve seals are removed. The heads are hot tanked and cleaned, and then Magnafluxed and pressure tested to check for any cracks, warping, or flaws in the casting. If the head is deemed a good candidate for a rebuild, the valves, guides, and seats are reground to factory spec, and the head is assembled.

A proper valve job is important for any rebuild because if you don't get a good valve seal the combustion process isn't efficient, and engine power is diminished. For a high-performance street car or dedicated race car, this is absolutely essential. The goal of a first-class valve job is to perfect the seal between the valve and the seat, and improve flow through them.

Some hot rodders are capable of doing a valve job on their favorite Chrysler street machine, and have access to the proper machinery and tools to perform the task. Most enthusiasts, however, do not have the tools or the training to properly perform a multi-angle valve job and instead need to have a capable machine shop rebuild the heads. If you want to disassemble the heads prior to sending them out to the machine shop, you can deliver them "bare" (without any valvetrain components). Either way, make sure to clean the heads with solvent and an enthusiastic scrubbing before taking them to the machine shop, taking the time to look for obvious cracks or damage. The machine shop hot tanks and washes the heads in solvent prior to their disassembly and inspection.

Check Valveguides

Unless you are having some optional (and expensive) head porting work done by your machine shop, the first step in rebuilding the heads is to check the valveguides. You are very likely to find that the valveguides are worn, tapered, or enlarged beyond spec. The way to check them is to drop the intake valve down the guide approximately 1/2 inch from the valve seat, and then measure the side-to-side movement of the valve head. Based on the .001- to .003-inch maximum valvestem-to-guide clearance spec from Chrysler for the intake valve (the exhaust valvestem-to-guide clearance must be .002 to .004 inch), that side-to-side movement of the intake valve head should be no more than .017 inch.

The most accurate way to check valveguide wear is to use a small hole gauge, which expands to fit the hole being measured. The gauge is removed from the hole and an outside micrometer is used to get the measurement. Whatever method you use to check the valveguides, if they are worn, they must be repaired. The most common fix is to enlarge the valveguide and fit it with either a K Line bronze guide insert or a Winona bronzewall guide insert.

Remove Valvetrain and Hardware

1 Remove Keepers, Retainers and Springs

With the spring compressed, you can remove the spring keepers by hand. If the keepers do not loosen when the spring is compressed, use a ballpeen hammer and tap the spring. If the keepers are a bit stubborn, lightly tap the spring in various places until they are free. Springs are removed and set aside for inspection.

2 Remove Valve Seals

You can remove valve seals with either a screwdriver or a pair of pliers. If you are saving the valves for a rebuild, use a pliers to remove the valve seals, being careful not to mar the valvestem.

3 File Valvestems

These rocker arms have hammered the tip of the valvestems for a long time, and as a result, the tip of the stem has mushroomed. In order to remove the valve without gouging the valveguide, file down the stem. You can then remove the valve. Repeat the process for all other valves. Unfortunately, filing down the tip calls for new valves.

Clean Cylinder Heads and Install Valveguides

1 Clean Heads

Machine shops use different methods for cleaning a core cylinder head. Various media may be used to do the initial cleaning, though care must be taken to not damage the heads in the process. These heads were cleaned in the jet cleaner, and then scrubbed with solvent and inspected. If the process is not satisfactory, it is repeated. Some shops use media blasting or a thermal cleaning process. Both will effectively clean the heads.

2 Deck Heads

These cylinder heads were set up on a decking machine to receive a surface cut in order to remove any imperfections or high spots along the surface of the heads, for the best possible seal during assembly. The procedure is similar to milling the heads, which takes off more metal for the purpose of increasing compression.

3 Press Valveguides

Rocker arms, moving in an upward and downward motion, actuate the intake and exhaust valves. The valvestem travels up and down in a machined cylinder, which is the valveguide. Unfortunately, the valves not only move up and down, they also rock slightly sideways. Over time, the valveguide wears. Worn guides result in increased oil consumption and allow air to be drawn into the intake ports, producing a lean condition. Rebuilding a cylinder head includes repairing the valveguide so that a tight seal is restored. The standard method for repairing valveguides involves reaming the valveguide and installing a valveguide insert that is tailored to the stem size of the valve. K-Line bronze valveguide liners provide excellent durability and performance.

The process of installing K-Line bronze valveguide inserts, or liners, is fairly straightforward for Jim Lewis. He owns a K-Line Carbide Boring Tool with a high-RPM (2,100 to be exact) air drill that is used to bore out the original valveguide. How does the boring tool accomplish this task with proper alignment to the valveguide? A K-Line valve seat bushing rests in the valve seat to provide the exact target for the boring tool. The boring tool is held in one hand, while the valve seat busing is held in the valve seat with the other hand. The valveguide is then bored.

4 Clean Shavings

After the guide has been bored, the shavings from the boring are blown or brushed away with compressed air. It is important to remove all shavings and chips from the valveguide and surrounding area.

5 Choose Valve Insert

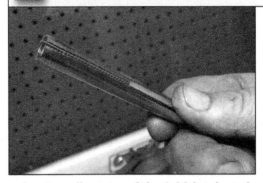

Each application requires the proper size bore and insert. Those sizes are determined by the valvestem diameter and the stem-to-guide clearance that is called for by the factory. For my application, the valvestem diameter of the 2.08 intake valve in this 915 head is .372 to .373 inch, with a stem-to-guide clearance of .001 to .003. Based on those specs, a 3/8-inch bronze insert is used.

6 Install Insert

The K-Line bronze valveguide insert is placed in the holder assembly of the K-Line Air Hammer. Once properly positioned, the air hammer drives the bronze insert into place.

7 Size Valveguide Inserts

The valveguide is installed, but now it must be properly sized to the newly bored valveguide in order to stay in place. A K-Line ball broach is dabbed with some K-Line lube, and attached to the air hammer.

8 Install Valveguide Inserts

The ball broach tool is run up and down in the guide to complete installation of the insert. The ball broach effectively slides the insert into the valveguide. This ball broach wedges, or mashes, the insert into the guide. It makes the insert bigger by about .0005 inch in the process.

9 Remove Excess Material

At this point, the cylinder head is turned over. Immediately apparent is the excess material from the newly installed valveguide inserts. A K Line Deluxe cutter is specifically designed to remove material from the valveguide inserts.

10 Prep for Teflon Seals

The top of the guides are cut down to prepare for the eventual installation of the Teflon valve seals. Cutters are matched to the size of the insert, and the excess material is removed.

11 Hone Inserts

Next, the bronze valveguide inserts are honed to provide proper stem-to-guide clearance.

Professional Mechanic Tip **PRO TIP**

12 Install Valveguide Pilot

Engine builders have preferences as to a method for cutting the seats. Some use a cutter, others use grinding stones. Jim uses a cutter on the exhaust seat and grinding stones on the intake as he is able to make finer adjustments with the stones. A pilot is installed in the valveguide because the valve seat must be concentric to the guide. The valve seat is ground while centered on the valveguide.

Perform Multi-Angle Valve Job

1 Use Three-Angle Valve Job

Grinding stones of various angles are used, depending on the desired angle on the seat. For the heads in this rebuild, we are going with a three-angle valve job. The exhaust seats receive three cuts. The top cut (closest to the combustion chamber) receives a 35-degree cut, the seat is cut at 45 degrees, and the bottom cut (cloest to the bowl) is radiused, or "rounded out."

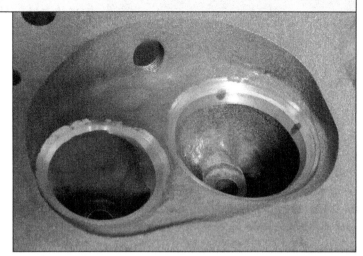

The intake valve seat gets a 35-degree top cut, 45-degree cut at the seat, and a 60-degree bottom cut. The width of the seat is .060. Though some prefer a shorter seat for racing, Lewis believes that the higher valvespring pressure needs a .060 seat, and that anything shorter only makes the seat burn up faster.

2 Touch-Up Valve Seat

Stones can be used to touch up the valve seat while testing for optimal flow. Numbers are run to determine if a quick grind on a seat results in better flow for the head.

3 Grind 45-Degree Face

Countless hours are spent tweaking the valve face and carefully grinding the seat for the best valve-to-seat seal. The 45-degree valve face that meets the valve seat is ground on this valve grinder. The valve rotates against the rotation of the high-speed grinding wheel. Oil is poured on the valve as the cut is made in order to wash away the residual grit and shavings. These small differences add up to a performance difference on the race track.

The "margin" on the valve is the area that is 90 degrees from the valve face. The margin on an intake valve is typically .050 inch, while the exhaust valve needs .080 to .100 for proper heat dissipation. The 45-degree cut is next, and then the 30-degree backcut on the inside of the 45-degree cut. That simple backcut helps create a significant power increase on both the intake and exhaust valves because it brings about improved flow, especially at low lift.

Install Valvetrain and Hardware

1 Clean Heads

After the valve seats have been cut, the head is again thoroughly washed and scrubbed to avoid any buildup of grit or shavings. Shops often wash and scrub the cylinder head while it is being rebuilt. Look for that kind of commitment to cleanliness when shopping for an engine builder.

2 Select Rocker Arm

There are a number of rocker arm options for the Mopar B and RB engines for high-performance street and other racing applications. Comp Cams offers roller rocker arms that provide greater strength and are an ideal choice for a higher lift cam, as well as an increased rocker arm ratio. The Comp Cams Ultra Pro Magnum roller rocker arms are made of chrome-moly and allow conversion from the shaft-mounted design to the steel stud mount. In addition, Comp Cams also offers a shaft-mounted aluminum roller rocker system that delivers far greater rigidity, and therefore improved efficiency and stability than the stock iron rockers. Both types of roller rockers are suited to a 600-hp rebuild.

For NHRA Stock Eliminator, aftermarket rocker arms are not legal, unless they are replacement rockers similar in design to the OEM units. Isky rockers (bottom) are made from iron, like the OEM rockers (top), and are legal for usage in NHRA Stock Eliminator racing. Therefore, for this build, we are using the Isky rocker arms.

Precision Measurement

3 Check Valvespring Clearance

According to Comp Cams, when the valve is fully open, the installed valvespring must have a minimum of .060-inch clearance between the coils to avoid coil bind. If clearance is not up to spec, the retainer, valvespring, or valve itself must be changed. The spring is compressed to the installed height, the valvespring pressure is measured, and the number is recorded. The spring is then compressed to the length at maximum valve lift to simulate the valve fully open, and that number is recorded. On a street car, the maximum lift must be .100 away from coil bind, while a race car ought to have .060 clearance between maximum lift and coil bind.

4 Fine-Tune Heads

Jim Lewis spent many hours on these heads to optimize flow within the boundaries of the rules of NHRA Stock Eliminator. The Super Flow SF-600 measures the flow in both intake and exhaust ports. The slightest change in the seats could bring about a significant improvement or loss in flow. While making cuts, the experienced worker knows not to cut too much from the head. As material is removed, the seat sinks farther into the head and deeper into the port.

5 Check Clearance

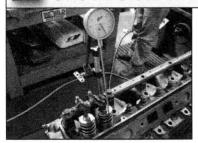

The head is about to be placed on the block to check for valve-to-piston clearance. With the head on the block and the degree wheel on the crank, the machinist rotates the crank clockwise while looking through the port at the valve chasing the piston down in its travel. At the closest visual point of the valve hitting the piston, he zeroes the dial indicator. He screws down the adjusting screw until the valve touches the piston, reads the number on the dial indicator, and writes it down. This is the first reading.

He backs out the adjusting screw so the valve goes to zero on the dial indicator. Then, he moves the crank clockwise 4 degrees, and zeros the dial indicator. He screws down the adjusting screw again until the valve again touches the piston. He records that number. It is the second reading. If the second reading is greater than the first reading, the machinist turns the crank counterclockwise 8 degrees. He zeroes the dial indicator, screws down the adjusting screw so the valve again touches the piston. He records that number. It is the third reading. If the third number on the dial indicator is smaller than the second reading, he moves the crank counter clockwise again another 4 degrees, zeroes the dial indicator, and screws down the adjusting screw until the valve touches the piston. He records the number as the fourth reading. If the fourth number is smaller than the third reading, he continues to turn the crank counterclockwise. If the fourth number is greater than the third reading, he has passed the smallest point of clearance between the piston valve. Therefore, he turns the crank clockwise back to where the closest point was, and checks it again.

In the hunt for the exact number, and to be more precise, he turns the crank counterclockwise 2 degrees, and repeats the process. The smallest number is the piston-to-valve clearance. It needs to be at least .060 inch for the intake. The process is repeated for the exhaust valve, remembering that the piston is coming up, chasing the exhaust valve as he turns the engine clockwise. Piston-to-valve clearance for the exhaust needs to be .100 inch.

Precision Measurement

6 Measure Combustion Chamber

With the valves, valvesprings, and spark plugs installed, the machinist uses Vaseline and a plexiglass plate to temporarily seal the combustion chamber. He uses a graduated burrette (in cubic centimeters) and rubbing alcohol to "pour" the chambers. (In order to easily see the alcohol in the burrette, he uses food coloring to ease visibility for measuring.) He slowly releases the alcohol from the burrette, and allows it to completely fill the chamber. He measures the amount of liquid in the chambers. That number is the volume of the combustion chambers. The eight chambers in these 915 heads were untouched, and varied from 75.2 to 76.8 cc.

Precision Measurement

7 Measure Installed Spring Height

The installed spring height is the distance from the bottom of the retainer to the area where the spring rests on the cylinder head. The machinist inserts the valve into the guide, slides a micrometer over the valvestem, and installs the retainer and locks. He records the micrometer measurement. The shortest installed height becomes the standard measurement for the other valves, and he uses shims to attain the same height, +/- .020 inch. Although the springs have not been installed, he measures the distance from the bottom of the retainer to the top of the valve seal. That distance cannot be greater than the valve lift, or severe valvetrain damage occurs.

8 Install Teflon Seals

The machinist places a coat of engine oil on the valvestem and on the Teflon insert in the seal. He uses the installation tool that looks like a tube or drinking straw. He places it through the center of the Teflon seal. With the Teflon seal right side up, he slides the tube over the valvestem, and then slides the Teflon seal over the valvestem. He pushes the seal over the valveguide until the metal retainer ring on the seal is fully engaged. Once the seals have been installed, they cannot be reused.

9 Insert Valve

He puts some engine oil on the intake valve of cylinder number-1, and inserts the valve. He places the valvespring on the seat and installs the retainer on the tip of the valvestem. Using a valvespring compressor, he compresses the spring and installs the pair of valve locks on the ends of the valves, making to sure they install properly. He releases the pressure on the spring. The retainer and locks should stay in place. The process is repeated for all of the other 15 valves.

10 Install Valve Retainer and Keeper

The machinist uses the valve spring compressor to install the retainer and keeper. He gives the heads a quick coat of engine paint and puts them aside until final engine assembly.

11 Beehive Springs

Comp Cams Beehive springs allow the engine to run less valvespring pressure while achieving higher RPM range. Less valvespring pressure means less stress on the lifters, pushrods, rocker arms, and all other valvetrain hardware, making valvetrain breakage less likely. The tapered shape and lighter material of the beehive spring and retainer help to reduce weight and avoid valve float in higher RPM ranges. Measurable gains have been seen above 6,300 rpm. Actual on-track testing is the real proof, but many street and race car owners are seeing power gains with these springs.

1966 "915" Cylinder Heads Specs

Valve to Deck Clearance	Intake .195 inch, Exhaust .230 inch
Combustion Chambers	75.2 to 76.8 cc (NHRA rule minimum 73.5 cc)
Intake Runners	189.4 to 193.6 cc (NHRA rule maximum 203 cc)
Exhaust Runners	59 to 60.4 cc (NHRA rule maximum 64 cc)
Intake Valve (2.08) Weight	120 grams
Exhaust Valve (1.60) Weight	96 grams
Retainer and Lock Weight	17 grams (OEM is 27 grams)
Intake Spring Height	1.775 inches
Valvespring Pressure	220 pounds on the seat, 430 pounds open at .435 lift

Flow Bench Results

Intake Lift (inch)	CFM	Exhaust Lift (inch)	CFM
.050	33	.050	30
.100	65	.100	57
.150	101	.150	84
.200	136	.200	100
.250	163	.250	113
.300	189	.300	125
.350	209	.350	134
.400	220	.400	140
.425	222	.437	143

CLEANING YOUR MACHINED PARTS

It would be interesting to know how many freshly machined engine components were assembled with the assumption that the machine shop did all the cleaning operations on the engine block, cylinder heads, crankshaft, and piston/rod assemblies, only to have an engine failure because of contaminants or blocked oil passages. Be sure your machine shop takes the time to explain to you what has been done (and not done) to your engine parts.

You have probably concluded that cleaning the machined components is your job. Machine shops know that most owners prefer to work on those parts themselves. The shop simply pre-assembles the engine and works with the parts to make sure the components correctly fit and to verify that the machine work has been properly performed. This is in preparation for final assembly so no parts suffer premature failure. Frankly, most shop owners probably believe they are doing the engine owner a favor by not completely washing the newly machined components because it saves the engine owner some money.

If your cam bearings have already been installed, check with your engine builder as to whether special care needs to be taken when washing and degreasing the block. Ask about cleaning and scrubbing, as he may know something about the particular components in your engine that are vulnerable to certain cleaning chemicals. Pull from him any information he has about prepping the block for final assembly.

A brand-new engine does not want to deal with foreign particles, metal shavings, or residual machining oil and solvent. The thrill of that first startup of your freshly rebuilt engine is largely dependent on how closely you and your machinist have paid attention to the details. Cleaning the block and other components is one of those huge payoffs that makes the hard work worth it.

Work Area and Helpers

All the components to be reused in your rebuild need to be cleaned and properly prepared for installation. Unless you are having the engine builder take care of the whole engine rebuild, you will handle the cleanup prior to final assembly.

The parts that come back from the machine shop are likely covered with some type of honing oil or cutting oil used during the various reconditioning steps. A number of machine shops spray components with oils or rust inhibitors (like WD-40) to keep certain parts from rusting. Newly bored and honed cylinder walls begin rusting immediately if exposed to the air, especially in a high-humidity climate. Whatever has been sprayed on your parts, you must now remove and properly clean and prep the engine block and components for final assembly.

It's always nice to have a second pair of hands. So why not have a buddy or two come over to assist you on this task? Make sure they have the same commitment to cleanliness and meticulous cleaning that you now have. If the person you have in mind to help you is impatient, a mechanical butcher, or a sloppy worker who is content with "good enough," look for someone else.

This process of cleaning and prepping requires the fine balance of speedy work with intense attention paid to detail. When helpers arrive, explain the process and plan of attack so they are aware of your expectations. It's your show, but assigning each person to a particular area of washing/scrubbing, or even a particular task of washing, can prove to be very efficient in getting your engine cleaned properly.

Before you begin, place the block on an engine stand that fully rotates for ease of access while cleaning. A pan located underneath the engine is the way to go, unless you are able to position the stand over some type of industrial drain.

Basic Cleaning Supplies

Make sure you have all supplies needed for the engine cleanup. The process for the final cleanup can be simplified to the following steps: degrease with degreaser, scrub with soapy water, dry with compressed air and towels, and protect with 10W-30 motor oil. If you pause for a trip to the parts store once the process begins, you must start the wash over, and possibly risk damage to newly machined surfaces.

Have at least three rolls of shop towels on hand, both blue and white. The towels must be lint free so as not to leave any particles behind on internal components. Either place them in close proximity to your parts washer, or have a 5-gallon bucket of solvent on hand for washing small parts.

Degreasing the engine requires about five cans of a degreaser of your choice. A number of builders use Simple Green, available in bulk at stores such as Walmart, which works very well. A number of builders also use Castrol Super Clean. If you are torn, buy both products and test them. Your engine builder is also a good source of information on this topic.

Rust begins when drying begins, so time is of the essence here. Dry the parts with compressed air and some lint-free towels. Immediately apply 10W-30 motor oil with other lint-free towels already soaked in oil. Use the towels to work the oil into the cylinder bores. Continue until you see no residue of any dirt, grime, or contaminants on the towels.

Some builders use automatic transmission fluid for this step followed by motor oil. The thinking is that it is more helpful in removing any residual honing oils or grit on the cylinders. I prefer to stick with motor oil only.

Because of the importance of the cylinders being fully protected, be extremely conscientious to work the oil into the bores. Having an extra helper or two speeds up this process to protect your cylinders.

Deep Cleaning

There are many ways to clean engines, including acid bathing, complete washing, and media blasting. (Keep in mind that you must not use steel, sand, or glass, which are abrasive medias, because they damage the components. In addition, these media types stick to the parts and are almost impossible to remove. If they leave the parts during engine operation, they cause engine damage and possibly outright failure.)

Many shops use ultrasonic cleaning. This process uses sound waves and a soapy mixture to thoroughly strip off the years of built-up oil, grease, and dirt. This method impeccably cleans the block and all components, which makes identifying damage, defects, and other problems much easier. If you choose ultrasonic cleaning, you need to take your engine to a professional machine shop.

If you opt to clean the engine by washing it yourself, use the following procedure.

Begin Cleaning

1 Prevent Rust

As the block and other components are cleaned and the various oils and solvents are washed off the metal, rust appears immediately. The cylinder walls are especially vulnerable during this time, so they need to be quickly protected with WD-40. Other areas on the block are equally susceptible to rust, such as the lifter bores and main bearing saddles.

You can be washing one side of the engine, and the other bank of cylinders rusts the moment it begins drying. You can retard rust formation by using a more concentrated mix of soap in the scrubbing water, but more effective is to limit the size of the area being washed. Also scrubbing one cylinder wall at a time helps avoid the unwanted appearance of rust.

2 Clean Hidden Areas

Set the block in an area with plenty of room for flying debris and use your power sprayer to completely soak it with degreaser. Remember to avoid direct contact of the degreaser with your cam bearings. Continue shooting solvent into areas to work out grime. Use the various brushes to clean all areas.

3 Clean All Holes

With all oil galley plugs removed, brush the passages with rifle brushes and various engine-cleaning brushes. Use plenty of degreaser until all oil passages are clear. Take time to check every one by inserting wires for inspection, or sometimes by shining a small, powerful flashlight through the passage.

4 Pressure-Wash Block

A large cabinet to shield flying spray and debris is extremely valuable for indoor cleaning. A hot-water supply aids in removing crud from the block. Focus on hidden deposits of grime and shoot the pressure washer into all crevices and galleys. After rinsing, repeat the process of applying solvent.

5 Remove Solvent

The block is attacked by the pressure wash in all holes, crevices, and newly machined surfaces.

All of the solvent must be removed from the block and replaced by WD-40 and engine oil.

6 Clean Cylinder Walls and Block

Use a soft brush for scrubbing with soapy water. Go over areas a number of times to remove every abrasive particle on those cylinder walls. Check to see progress using compressed air to dry, and rub a clean but oiled white rag along the cylinder walls. Any trace of black hone residue means you have more scrubbing to do. When the white rag finally turns up clean, scrub it some more, and then dry everything with air and rags.

Scrub the block both internally and externally. Feel along the walls, internal webbing, and cylinder walls. As mentioned, oily residue means more cleaning and scrubbing. Once the block seems free of that oily substance, scrub some more, and prepare to protect your block with WD-40 and engine oil.

7 Dry Components Completely

Grab your air hose, and get to drying the engine completely. Shoot all crevices, oil galleys, water coolant passages, and bolt holes with compressed air. Spin the block on the stand at 90-degree increments, and keep blasting the block with air.

8 Lubricate Engine Components

Once the engine has been degreased, washed, scrubbed, and dried, it's time to apply WD-40 to all surfaces of the engine that must be protected from rust. Deck, lifter bores, oil pump mating surface, main bearing saddles, and any other finished area needs to be completely covered and protected with oil. Use lint-free rags, just for insurance.

9 Clean and Prep Other Major Components

Pay special attention to the crankshaft throws, to rid them of accumulated grease and grime. After using the engine brush to clear all oiling holes, scrub the crank with soapy water, similar to how you cleaned the block. Our heads were already cleaned and set aside for assembly, but the intake manifold was in need of attention. The intake manifold was treated to a thorough washing, and then a soapy-water scrubbing to get it thoroughly clean. Use engine oil along the cylinder head mating surface, stopping any rust formation. Some parts such as the exhaust manifold need to be bead blasted prior to washing. Other parts such as the thermostat housing, water pump, and various fittings need cleaning.

10 Clean Main Caps and Rear Main Seal Cap

The rear main seal is a difficult component to clean, as the rubber seal leaves residue. Not only was this rear main seal retainer cap cleaned, it was scrubbed. And it had to be scraped with a knife in the areas where the rubber had welded itself to the retainer. Be very careful to avoid gouging the cap during cleaning, but be thorough in providing a clean surface for the new rear main seal.

11 Clean Smaller Parts

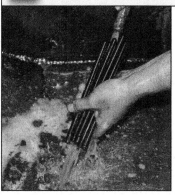

The small parts that you have set aside to be used again need to be cleaned, such as brackets, clamps, and mounts. Use the same methods as you used on the larger components so you enter the assembly process with all parts prepped and clean.

12 Replace Oil Plugs

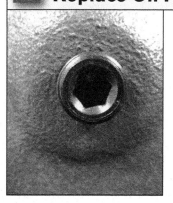

All the oil galley plugs that were removed need to be replaced. Pipe plugs, however, might be installed later, depending on accessibility. When you do replace them, do not use Teflon tape. Rather, use a light coating of pipe thread sealant to provide a reliable seal.

PRE-ASSEMBLY

Before assembling the engine, take an inventory of parts to make sure all necessary components are present and accounted for. The machined block and all components must be properly prepared and clean. Keep in mind the overarching concept at this stage of the engine rebuild is a pre-assembly, or mock-up, process.

Pre-assembling and then assembling the engine is an exacting and meticulous process requiring great attention to detail so the engine is balanced and running at its best. Throwing together a skid load of parts that produces an engine that runs "okay" is worlds apart from the effort needed to build an engine that is reliable, efficient, and powerful. Focus on how these newly purchased or machined parts work together. All specifications and measurements must be met, and therefore all parts must fit correctly. To perform at optimum level, parts must support and complement the entire package.

I grew up hearing about engines that were blueprinted—built with perfection as the goal. Now there is certainly no such thing as the perfect engine, but that is always the goal.

Part of careful engine assembly involves blueprinting various parts to make sure they fit properly prior to their final installation. For example, the main caps and crankshaft are installed a number of times for various reasons prior to their final installation. Check factory clearances, torque specs, fastener tightening sequences, valvetrain events, and cam timing specs.

Engine Notebook

If you don't already have one, now is the time to get a notebook to record every part number, casting number, clearance number, torque setting, ring gap, piston-to-valve clearance, and cam timing information. Have it handy in order to take notes of measurements and clearances as the engine is assembled. There are a number of calculations necessary, so also have a calculator or computer available.

By the way, don't skip the note-book thinking you can just remember all the information and enter it directly into your computer. That computer might not be accessible.

The data you jot down in your notebook is invaluable reference information for both tuning and diagnostics. Make note of the actual numbers, not the ones that your engine is supposed to produce. As the build progresses, a problem might develop that could be traced to a particular event in the assembly. The only way to discover a wrong turn is to be able to check the book to recall your assembly procedures and results.

Tools

In Chapter 2, I discuss the tools necessary for an engine rebuild, and now those tools must be laid out in an organized manner, with easy accessibility.

The process of degreeing your cam calls for a degree wheel, a dial indicator with a magnetic base, a wire for creating a pointer, and a crank nut and bolt that allows the

Fastener Torque Specs

A number of the fasteners that are used in the construction of an engine must be tightened a certain amount. In other words, you do not rebuild an engine properly by haphazardly tightening all the bolts as tight as you can.

Use a torque wrench to tighten a number of the critical fasteners a certain amount in order to provide equal pressure or clamping force to the component being installed. Also use a torque wrench to tighten the main bearing cap bolts, the connecting rod bolts, head bolts, and most other fasteners to the proper specifications.

NOTE: These torque specs are provided for a reference only. Different assembly lubricants can affect and therefore change the final torque spec. Without exception, always reference ARP's or the manufacturer's fastener torque specs and instructions. Follow them accordingly.

Engine Part/Component	Stock Bolts/OEM Spec (ft-lbs)	ARP Bolts/Ultra Torque Lube (ft-lbs)
Main Bearing Caps	85	100
Connecting Rod Bolts	45	55
Head bolts	70	80
A/C Compressor Engine Bolt	30	30
Balancer Bolt	135	135
Camshaft Locking Bolt	35	35
Carb to Intake Nut	7	7
Distributor Clamp	15	15
Exhaust Manifold Nut	30	30
Flywheel/Flexplate to Crank	55	55
Intake Manifold	40	40
Oil Pan	15	15
Oil Pump Cover	10	10
Oil Pump	35	35
Rear Main Seal Retainer	30	30
Rocker Shaft Brackets	25	25
Starter Mounting Bolts	50	50
Timing Cover	15	15
Valley Pan End Bolt	9	9
Water Pump	30	30

crankshaft to be rotated both clockwise and counterclockwise.

To pre-assemble the piston and rings package you need micrometers, a dial bore gauge, a dial caliper gauge, a dial indicator, a straightedge, various feeler gauges, a ring grinder, machinist files, and some emery paper.

To make installation a clean, simple task, you need a piston ring compressor, possibly a piston ring expander, and a ring-squaring tool.

You need access to a distributor bushing installation tool.

Also, have at least two pairs of rod bolt protectors and a strong but small flashlight close at hand.

Many tools are available for rent at your local parts store; some might even be available at no charge.

Supplies

By now you have a pretty good feel for the necessary "staples" of shop supplies, so look around your shop/garage, and make sure you are prepared.

Have plenty of lint-free shop towels on hand.

You also need basic supplies for cleaning, solvent or thinner, motor oil, and ARP assembly lube or similar.

You need at least three to five packages of Plastigage (.001 to .003 inch) for checking main bearing and rod bearing clearances.

Cam lube for cam break-in must be on hand soon for final assembly, as well as gasket sealer, tubes of silicone, and copper gasket spray.

Preparing to Rebuild Cylinder Block

The freshly machined and cleaned cylinder block must be positioned properly, either on an engine stand or a proper machinist's table, depending on the preferences of your engine builder. Every crevice, all threaded holes, and oil passage holes must be perfectly clean. When all looks good, freeze plugs and cam bearings can be installed.

Block Preparation

Critical Inspection

1 Prep Block

Examine the bare block before you begin. Make sure it is secure on the engine stand, and that it rotates easily.

Even though the machine shop has the responsibility to clean all the parts after the engine has been machined, it doesn't mean mistakes cannot be made. Therefore, you need to thoroughly wash the block and remove any particles or sediment that could damage the internal components of the engine. Apply solvent and scrub every surface and passage of the engine and then pressure wash the block to make sure all debris has been removed. Make sure the solvent does not leave residue behind.

Chase each threaded hole and lubricate the threads with a tap. Use lint-free towels and pressurized air to dry the block. And coat the surfaces with oil or WD-40 so they don't rust.

2 Install Brass Freeze Plugs

Any engine rebuild must receive new freeze plugs (sometimes referred to as Welch plugs), no matter how clean and solid the old ones appear to be. The factory used steel freeze plugs that can rust. Most builders use brass freeze plugs that do not rust and ultimately are more reliable than steel units.

Use a gasket sealant, such as NAPA High Tack Gasket Sealant, and apply as directed. When the gasket sealant is ready (slightly tacky), place the new brass freeze plugs in the hole. Lightly tap the freeze plug with a hammer to get it started in the hole, but avoid using the hammer to drive the freeze plug into the hole, since it could very easily damage the flanged outer edge of the plug.

Once you have the freeze plug started, find a socket and extension to fit inside the freeze plug, and gently tap the extension. Allow the freeze plug to enter the hole until the flanged edge lands just below the chamfered edge of the block.

Wipe off any excess sealant from the plug and the block. (Other plugs will be installed after the block has been painted.)

3 Ensure Oil Supply

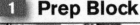

All oil passages were cleared of blockages and obstructions during the cleaning process. Additionally the holes in the saddles were chamfered in order to ensure proper oil supply to the main bearings.

4 Install Cam Bearings

Cam bearings must be replaced to perform a proper engine rebuild. Not only are they likely to have significant wear, they have also been subjected to hot tanking at the machine shop. That process alone is enough to justify the replacement of the cam bearings.

For our 383 rebuild, Dura-Bond camshaft bearings were used. Even though the camshaft journals are all the same size, the five camshaft bearing bores in the block are different sizes. Therefore, each cam bearing is a different size corresponding to the cam bearing bore in the block.

Make absolutely sure that you are installing bearings in the proper position. Each bearing has a hole that must match up with the oil galley in the main bearing saddle. Inspect the bearings, one at a time, and make sure the bearings are not damaged or nicked in any way.

4 Install Cam Bearings *CONTINUED*

Once the bearing is in the proper alignment, use a hammer to install the bearing. Here's a close look at the care needed to guide the cam bearings into proper position. You can see how the installation tool holds the bearings in place on the arbor.

The cam bearing installation tool essentially holds the cam bearings while you precisely align the bearing with the oil feed hole on the main bearing saddles.

Make a line on the outside wall of the bearing, marking the oil hole location in order to ensure that the bearing does not turn while being installed. If the bearing turns, the oil hole in the bearing is out of alignment, and the oil flow is partially or completely blocked.

Main Bearings and Caps Installation

The main bore must be within spec. The main bearings must be installed and the main caps torqued to spec. A dial bore gauge is necessary to carefully measure the main bore in order to confirm proper clearances for crankshaft rotation. Remember to record all measurements in your engine notebook. Final prep and detailing of the surfaces will pay big dividends for the reliability and longevity of your new motor.

Performance Tip

1 Check Main Bore

The first order of business is to check the main bore. If the block is currently top side up, turn it over so the bottom side is facing up. If the main bearing bores are not prepped correctly, the entire rotating assembly is crippled.

Use a shop towel to clean the main bearing saddles in the block. The main caps must also be cleaned with a paper towel. Next, install the caps to the main saddles without the bearings. Use ARP Ultra Torque Assembly Lube on the ARP main cap bolts. Apply a thin coat to all contact surfaces, including the top and bottom of the washers, in order to provide a clean torque reading.

Torque Fasteners

2 Torque Main Cap Bolts

Stock main cap bolts are torqued to 85 ft-lbs; ARP main cap bolts call for 100 ft-lbs. Make sure you use the correct torque spec for the fasteners throughout the assembly process. The higher torque rating means stronger clamping power on the caps, which is a great benefit in any high-performance street engine, and especially in a race engine. Apply steady, smooth force as you tighten the bolts.

Standard practice when torquing any fastener calls for reaching spec by going through three equal increments of tightening using the factory torque sequence. For example, ARP main cap bolts must be torqued to 100 ft-lbs. Therefore, begin by torquing all bolts to 35 ft-lbs, then set the torque wrench to 70 ft-lbs and tighten, then put the setting at 100 ft-lbs and complete the task.

Precision Measurement

3 Measure Main Bore

As each cap is installed, use the dial bore indicator to measure the main bore. Checking the bore at multiple spots helps confirm that the bores are perfectly circular. (If not, the align hone or align bore work done is flawed and must be taken back to the machine shop.) Factory spec on the main bore is 2.625 inches.

4 Select and Clean Main Bearings

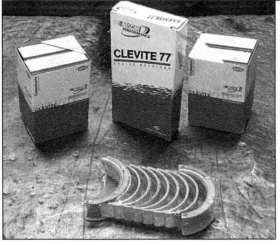

On a big-block Mopar, there are a number of opinions on the best main bearings to select. Some say to use grooved main bearings all around, while others make the case for grooved on the main saddles and non-grooved on the main caps. The issue revolves around the tendency of the crank to exit out the bottom of the engine under high-RPM loads. In other words, the main caps endure greater stress than the main bearing saddles in the block. A grooved bearing in the main caps is more likely to split at the groove because of that stress. For our rebuild, Jim Lewis chose grooved bearings all around.

5 Prepare Main Bearings

There are a number of detailing items necessary to prepare for the installation of the main bearings. With a piece of emery cloth lightly deburr any irregularities and slightly chamfer the edges of the main caps. Some engine builders use a fine file to clean up the edges, accomplishing essentially the same thing as the emery cloth. In preparation for inserting Plastigage, clean the bearing surface of any foreign particles. The bearings are also cleaned and readied for assembly and the clearance will be measured with Plastigage.

6 Install Main Bearings

Match the tang on the bearing to the notch in the cap to fit the main bearings onto the main caps. Fit the bearings into the caps, and then move them to make the surfaces flush with the cap. The bearings should easily slide into place.

7 Install Bearing Caps

With the main bearings installed in the saddles, the main caps with bearing must now be torqued down. Remember, factory bolts require 85 ft-lbs, while the ARP bolts require 100 ft-lbs. Use assembly lube on the bolts in order to produce accurate readings. Torque down the bolts in three stages. Once the caps have been installed, use the dial bore gauge to measure each bore. Record the measurements in your notebook. Once the bores have been checked and found to be within your spec, remove the caps in preparation for checking the bearing crush with Plastigage.

Main Bearing Crush Measurement

Measuring main bearing crush determines that the clearance between the crankshaft and main bearings is set to proper spec. The process includes working from the measurements recorded while checking the main bore, and then carefully measuring the crank jour-nals. Having measured and recorded those numbers, Plastigage is used to confirm that the clearance is within spec.

1 Measure Bearing Crush

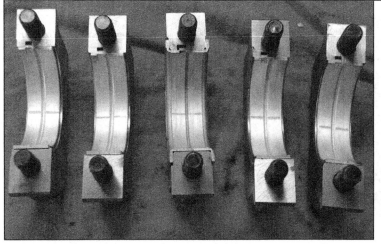

Lay the Plastigage across the areas that require clearance measurements. Here the Plastigage is laid across the main cap bearings. Note that the bearing is completely free of oil and dry. Any oil on the bearing produces a false reading.

With the Plastigage in place, lay the crank in the block. Do not spin the crank; simply lay it into the saddles. If the crank turns, it smears the Plastigage, and the process must be started over.

2 Apply Assembly Lubricant

Make sure there is a sufficient coverage of the ARP Fastener Assembly Lubricant on both the bolts and the washers for the main caps to accurately torque the caps to spec.

3 Clean Main Bearing Caps

The main caps must be clean prior to installing on the block for the Plastigage reading, with special attention paid to cleaning the contact areas on the caps. Apply a light coat of assembly lube on the contact surfaces to prevent any type of binding.

Torque Fasteners

4 Reinstall Main Bearing Caps

Although it may seem repetitive and tedious, the main cap bolts must be reinstalled for the purpose of examining bearing clearance.

With the bearing in the crank, place the main on the crank and properly torque the caps to 100 ft-lbs in three increments: 35-, 35-, and 30-ft-lbs. Do not install the rear main seal at this time. Do not turn the crank, or you need to start the process over. Once all the caps have been tightened, remove the caps.

5 Remove Main Bearing Caps

With the caps removed, keep them free of dirt and arranged in proper order. This is when Chrysler's procedure of casting the numbers of the caps into the caps themselves becomes good insurance for keeping them in their proper place.

6 Take Plastigage Measurements

While the cap is off, do not turn the crank. Use the package markings to measure the thickness of the crushed Plastigage. A tighter clearance crushes the Plastigage more, making it wider. The factory specs call for .0005- to .0015-inch clearance for the main bearings, which is excellent for a street car. For a free-spinning rotating assembly, the clearance target is about .002 inch.

Precision Measurement

7 Measure Main Bearing Cap Crush

Using the Plastigage wrapper, measure the width of the crushed Plastigage. It should measure between .0015 and .002 inch, all within clearances. When all measurements have been taken, use a rag to remove any trace of Plastigage from the surfaces. Clean the surfaces with motor oil and a lint-free paper towel.

Plastigage comes in this wrapper, which is marked for easy reading. The one you want to use is the one that measures from .001 to .003 inch, as clearly marked on the wrapper. Plastigage is simply a very thin piece of plastic that is laid on the surface that requires measurement. The amount that the Plastigage spreads after being crushed is the clearance measurement.

Connecting Rods Installation

Similar to checking the main bearing bore for crankshaft rotation clearances, the connecting rods must also be examined. The connecting rod bearings must be installed, and measurements must be confirmed of both the connecting rod bore and the crank journal. The difference is the clearance that must be within spec, and confirmed by using Plastigage. Remember to record all measurements in your engine notebook.

Precision Measurement

1 Check Connecting Rod Bore

Verify that the rod and main bearings are correctly matched so the bearings have the correct amount of crush. Place the rods in a soft-jaw vice. Lube the connecting rod bolts and torque down the connecting rod bolts to spec. Use an outside micrometer to measure the crankshaft journal diameter and a dial bore gauge to measure the connecting rod, but remember the bearings must be installed and the fasteners tightened to the manufacturer's recommended torque spec. The difference between the crank spec and the connecting rod spec should be the clearance available, which is confirmed by the Plastigage.

2 Check Connecting Rod Side Clearance

Measure the side clearance of the installed rod to confirm the amount of side clearance, which should be between .009 and .017 inch. The rods are held tightly together with the chamfered side of each rod facing outward. Slightly rotate each rod so the wrist pin bores are not touching and record the measurement. Use the caliper to measure the intended connecting rod journal on the crankshaft. The difference between those two numbers is the connecting rod side clearance.

Prepare to Install Crankshaft

It is critical to measure crankshaft endplay at this point. The crank must be able to move slightly while rotating. Factory spec for crank endplay is from .002 to .007 inch. If they are not found to be within spec, either the crankshaft thrust surfaces must be corrected or the crank thrust bearings must be modified. These corrections need to be made prior to the final balancing work on the rotating assembly.

Precision Measurement

1 Check Crankshaft Endplay

The main caps must again be installed and torqued down to check for crank endplay. You are measuring the effectiveness of the thrust bearing, and need to know that crank endplay ranges from .002 to .007 inch.

Crankshaft endplay was checked during disassembly for diagnostic purposes, and now it is time to check it again. Make sure the widths on the crankshaft thrust surfaces are correct. Mount the dial indicator on the block and position the tip on the crank snout. Using a large screwdriver, find a place to safely pry the crank forward and then "zero" the indicator. Move the crank to the rear of the engine. Move the crank forward again and "zero" the indicator again. According to the factory specs, the desired crankshaft endplay reading should be between .002 and .007 inch.

2 Select Pistons

Piston quality and production is at an all-time high. A number of piston manufacturers offer excellent products for enthusiasts to suit most budgets. There might be some of you who are using your original pistons, either because they had just been replaced, or because they were in excellent condition. However, most of you are working with a newly bored block that requires new pistons. Smart shoppers likely found a suitable engine kit from a mail-order company. The quality of these kits is often very good but the cheapest kits might be the ones to avoid, though not always. A medium-priced engine kit might contain a mixed bag of acceptable and unacceptable quality parts. As far as I'm concerned, M17s from CP Pistons are as good as any pistons, but they might be overkill for your street car. CP Pistons has the Bullet line of street pistons, typical of most piston manufacturers offering less expensive choices. CP pistons also call for a floating-pin arrangement, as opposed to the pressed-pin design that came from Chrysler. A pressed-pin design is completely acceptable on a street engine and is even being used on some race engines.

3 Measure Piston Bore Size

Jim Lewis measured the bore size of our CP pistons with a micrometer, and all eight were found to be spot-on perfect. He also used a digital vernier caliper to confirm proper ring groove locations, which also checked out exactly to spec.

*These pistons feature anti-detonation grooves, which protect the top ring by disrupting detonation waves and limiting the piston/cylinder contact during high-RPM usage. An accumulator groove is a V-shaped groove in the second ring land, which collects excess blow-by between the top and second ring. Ring seal is improved, and top ring flutter is virtu-*ally eliminated. *These pistons are designated M17 CP, which is stamped on the top of the piston and is also found on NHRA's list of accepted pistons for Stock Eliminator racing.*

Early 383 engines, like the one being built, feature closed-chamber heads, and the pistons have no dome and there-fore are flat-top pistons. All B and RB production pistons were offset, meaning that the piston pin was not centered in the piston. The reason for the offset piston was to make the engine quiet on cold starts.

Jim measures from the top of the ring to the top of the piston in order to make sure it is within NHRA specs. The reason for that rule is that the closer the first ring gets to the top of the piston, the more power it makes, since compression increases. NHRA says that the minimum distance from the top of the upper ring groove to the top of the piston must be .330 inch, and each piston came in at that number.

Piston Ring Installation

Cylinder sealing is an important aspect of increasing horsepower, and piston ring selection is crucial for optimizing cylinder pressure. Many engines are built with conventional pre-gapped piston rings that are ready for installation. A conventional ring set with end gap is a place for a leak path. The better the rings seal inside the cylinder and against the piston, the more air/fuel mixture enters the combustion chamber. A greater air/fuel mixture present in the chamber produces a more powerful combustion. The ability of the engine to draw in that air/fuel mixture is determined by how well the rings maintain cylinder seal and resultant cylinder pressure.

Conventional pre-gapped rings face the reality of the end gap closing because of expansion brought on by the heat of combustion. As the rings expand, the end gap narrows. If the end gap closes completely, the ring could lose its proper function and its ability to seal the cylinder. For that reason, end gaps are wider than you might want for maximum horsepower.

When seeking to gain the most power from an engine, there is much discussion about sealing the cylinder for optimum cylinder pressure. The task of sealing the cylinder falls to the piston rings. If you are rebuilding an engine for the street with pre-gapped piston ring sets, your task at this point is to simply install the rings on the pistons and then check the ring end gap. Usually, a pre-gapped set of rings arrives without any need for gapping, but they do need to be measured to verify claimed gap.

The top Seal ring is gapless, creating a total seal, with no end gap. This design increases cylinder pressure, which means greater power, fuel/air mixture velocity, and higher compression. Spacer with notches, gas porting gets behind the compression ring, and pushes it. The piston ring is a two-piece design with ring and secondary rail segment.

Many engine builders agree that benefits can be obtained with improved cylinder sealing during each of the four strokes of the internal combustion engine. As mentioned, a tighter cylinder seal improves the "vacuum" that draws the air/fuel mixture into the combustion chamber. On the compression stroke of the engine, a tighter engine seal lessens the amount of that air/fuel mixture escaping past the piston into the crankcase, resulting in increased force needed to compress the mixture. The power stroke in the engine that features greater cylinder seal experiences the explosion staying above the piston, resulting in a more powerful downward pressure on the piston. Finally, exhaust gases escape more speedily and efficiently if the cylinder seal is optimized.

I am installing a ring package in this 383 engine that's in compliance with the NHRA Stock Eliminator rules calling for pistons with grooves that have a 5/64-inch top ring, 5/64-inch second ring, and 3/16-inch oil ring. I am using a ring package from Total Seal that features a gapless top ring, low-drag Napier second ring, and low-tension oil ring.

The top ring of Total Seal's package is actually a two-piece design that features a main ring and an interlocking rail that closes the end gap. The rail in the piston groove deflects its compression, and therefore the ring itself is pushed against the cylinder walls for greater sealing and less blow-by during the four-stroke cycle. Further, whereas newly installed conventional rings can show leak-down numbers of 7 percent, newly installed gapless rings show leak-down numbers in the 2-percent range.

The two-piece gapless top ring could look confusing to someone who has only seen conventional end gap rings. This drag racing application calls for optimum cylinder pressure with minimal parasitic drag, making this choice ideal. A conventional ring package is more appropriate for a street engine, either stock or high performance.

Though designs differ, piston ring installation is fairly standard, as shown in the following procedure.

Install Piston Rings

Precision Measurement

1 Measure Ring Width

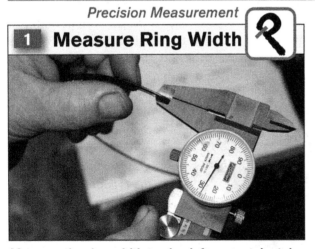

Measure the ring width to check for proper installation into the ring grooves. Use a digital vernier caliper to confirm proper ring width. Depending on your ring package, widths vary. Factory specs on a stock 1970 383 Mopar engine are listed as .0775 to .0780 inch for the first ring, .0775 to .0780 for the second ring, and .025 for the third ring.

Precision Measurement

2 Measure Piston Ring Gap

Soak a shop towel with engine oil. Use it to oil the cylinder walls. In order to gap the file fit rings, each ring must be placed square in the particular cylinder in which they are being installed and then measured with a feeler gauge.

After the ring is set in the cylinder, the top of the piston is used to locate the ring square to the cylinders. Factory recommendation for the ring end gap for the first and second ring is .013 to .023 inch. For the third ring, the oil ring, the factory end gap spec is .015 to .055. Remember, the ring end gap must fit your particular application. Check with the supplier, your machinist, or engine builder to decide on the gap for your application. If you are working with a custom ring set, the end gap of all three rings is most likely different, so keep all rings organized and labeled for each cylinder.

3 Gap Piston Rings

The rings need to be checked for end gap whether you are filing your own file-fit rings, having a machine shop do it for you, or installing pre-gapped rings.

Be sure to label the rings for each cylinder. After the ring has been placed in the cylinder, it must be squared in the bore using either a ring squaring tool or using your piston without any rings installed.

Once in the proper place, use a feeler gauge to measure the ring gap. Measure the gap when the ring is about 1 inch down in the hole, but then also check the gap as it nears the deck. The best place for final measurement is about 1 inch down in the cylinder.

As you are standing at the ring grinder with the handle jabbing you in the gut, turn the handle clockwise, so the ring pulls away from your hand.

(Note the lack of protective gloves in this photo; it would be better to have hand protection for this task).

Only file a small amount at a time. Frequently check the gap by placing the ring in the cylinder bore and measuring the gap with the feeler gauge. Any time a ring goes into the cylinder for measurement use a shop towel with engine oil to coat the cylinder walls, so the bore surfaces are lubricated and scratches on the walls are prevented. As the rings are file-fitted to the pistons and cylinders, keep them organized so they are not improperly assembled.

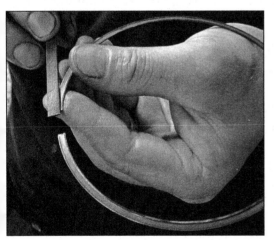

Filing the rings is a relatively time consuming and tedious job. When the ring gaps are where they need to be, take a fine machinist's file

and clean the edges of burrs or imperfections, but don't chamfer them. Improper ring gaps mean premature wear on the cylinder walls, less than optimal cylinder pressure, and premature ring failure. As the rings are filed, a free-spinning reciprocating assembly is the goal. You want the perfect balance of excellent ring seal to provide maximum vacuum on the intake stroke, and the seal for compression, but you also want the rings to give the least amount of resistance in the process.

The third ring from the top, called the oil ring, goes on the piston first. It is usually a three-piece arrangement, with two side

rails and a middle spacer, sometimes called the expander.

Do not use a ring expander (a tool that holds a ring in an expanded position for installation) to install the oil ring side rails as it could damage the rings. Working your way up the piston, add the second ring, then the ring closest to the top of the piston. Some builders use ring expanders to install the top two piston rings; others spiral the rings on the piston. Either way is acceptable.

4 Measure Rod Bore

Check the rod bore one more time prior to attaching the piston to the small end of the rod. If you are fortunate enough to have a rod bore gauge, such as this Sunnen Precision Gauge, simply put the rod in place on the gauge, and measure at 90-degree increments.

5 Install Connecting Rod and Piston

The tangs on the rods must face out. Line up the piston on the floating pin and work the snap rings, or pin locks, into place. They fit nicely in the groove of the piston and keep the pin in place.

Camshaft Installation

If any single component determines the power output and the characteristics of an engine, the camshaft is it. In plain language, the camshaft controls the opening and closing of the valves. It not only determines the timing of the valve's opening and closing, it also controls how long the valves stay open and how much distance they travel off the seat when opening.

Choosing the camshaft to suit your particular needs is a make-or-break decision. If you're rebuilding a bone-stock engine, you can install a factory-spec or OEM-type cam, and therefore you don't have to do any research to determine which cam is best for your combination. For higher-performance rebuilds, however, you need to select a cam that provides the correct lift, duration, and lobe separation for your valvetrain and engine in total. The choices are nearly infinite and every combination cannot be covered in this book.

Though choosing the right cam for your build is absolutely critical, keep in mind that you also need to properly install it; otherwise you could be faced with a complete disaster. For that reason, it is extremely helpful to learn some basics about what a camshaft does and how to correctly install one.

Camshaft Terminology

The cam must be compatible with your heads and valvetrain. Remember, you're assembling a compatible and complementary package, therefore the entire package must operate in harmony. To put together a compatible package, you need to understand cam timing events. (And it also helps you keep up with your engine builder, your buddies at the cruise night, or even your young son who is beginning to dig your car hobby.)

When it comes to cam timing, you do not have win-win or gain-gain changes or upgrades. In other words, if you gain in one area, you often lose in another. However, the more cam timing events you can determine for your engine package, the better chance you have of selecting the correct cam. Therefore, you need to consider all the specific components of the engine package to be sure that intake, heads, compression ratio, displacement, headers, fuel system, and carburetor or fuel injection all work together. As you investigate and decide upon the cam that best suits your car, application, and driving style, you will come to the realization that it's a balancing act to select the right cam.

To figure out the optimal cam and valve timing events for your particular package, you can refer to any of several online software programs that provide information for making a wise selection. For example, Comp Cams offers free downloadable software to accomplish this task.

The following are some concepts that will surely come up in your research.

Cam Phasing: This is the position of the camshaft in relation to the crankshaft and is critical to achieving optimum timing of the opening and closing of the valves with respect to the position of the piston.

Centerline: The camshaft centerline is the position of the cam in relation to the crankshaft.

Duration: This is how long a valve remains open in relation to the crankshaft rotation. The time period that the valve stays open is expressed in degrees of crankshaft rotation, and this largely determines the powerband of the engine.

Gross Valve Lift: This is the measurement in inches that the valve actually opens. To determine gross valve lift, multiply the advertised cam "lobe lift" by the rocker arm ratio. For example, the Comp Cams cam in this engine rebuild advertises a lobe lift of .2880 inch on the intake and exhaust lobes. The rocker arm ratio is 1.5:1. Therefore, you multiply .2880 by 1.5 to arrive at the .432 gross valve lift.

Gross valve lift is affected by valve lash, lifter bleed down, valvetrain deflection, and production tolerances in the rocker arms. Gross valve lift is essentially the maximum valve lift under ideal conditions. Since there are no ideal conditions, it becomes necessary to calculate "net valve lift."

Net Valve Lift: This is determined by subtracting the valve lash dimension from the gross valve lift measurement, but measuring net valve lift is the most precise method. However, in the typical valvetrain the other aforementioned variables exist. Again, these are lifter bleed down, valvetrain deflection, and production tolerances in the rocker arms.

Remember, the lifter pushes the pushrod, which pushes the "tail" of the rocker arm up. The "nose" of the rocker arm pushes the tip of the valvestem down. Understanding those terms helps you to arrive at net valve lift.

The best method to determine actual net valve lift in a non-running engine is to set up a dial indicator on the valve retainer, as close as possible to the nose of the rocker arm. The amount of travel is the net valve lift. Greater valvetrain stability aids the engine in achieving the maximum amount of net valve lift,

which in turn should help an engine achieve its greatest performance potential.

A valve that does not have much lift often produces good low-end torque but doesn't provide enough fuel at high RPM so it's often down on horsepower. A high-performance cam typically increases cam lift for high-RPM horsepower gain, but typically the engine doesn't produce good low-end torque.

But if you opt for a cam that increases the gross valve lift, you must use compatible heads, valves, and rocker arms. A higher-lift cam may actually be detrimental to performance if the combustion chamber is too small to accommodate the increase in cylinder filling. A greater amount of lift puts more distance between the valve and the seat, and this correlates into increased airflow. You can only increase valve lift so far before the valve starts coming into contact with the top of the piston.

1 Install Camshaft

Before degreeing your camshaft, you must first assemble the short block. Since the cam is installed for fitment and not final installation, simply coat the cam journals with engine oil. Apply oil to the cam bearings as well, a thin coat will do. Slowly and carefully guide the camshaft through the cam tunnel into the block, doing your best to go straight into the cam bearing bores without nicking or gouging the cam lobes.

You should have already confirmed that the camshaft spins freely in the cam bearings. If it does not, remove the cam to see if there are any burrs on the bearings that need to be touched up with emery paper. If there is a more serious situation, the block may have to go back to the machine shop to remove the cam bearings and install a new set. Use the lubricant recommended by the cam manufacturer.

Precision Measurement

2 Measure Rod Journal

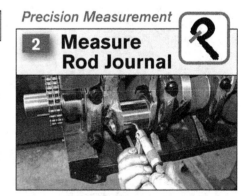

Before any connecting rods go on the rod journal, take another measurement. This particular crank was cut .010 (mains) and .020 (journals), so the measurements should reflect that machine work. The rod journals must all be the same. The caliper measures the main journal, and that measurement is transferred to a dial bore gauge to measure the rods.

3 Cover Connecting Rod Bolts

To protect your newly machined block, use Clevite rubber boots on the rod bolts to keep the bolts from scratching the cylinder walls and crankshaft during installation. If you don't have these sleeves handy, a section of rubber hose over the bolts suffices. The rods must go into the cylinder with the bearing tang facing the outside of the engine. The rods are built with a chamfered edge along the outside edge of the rod on one side only. That chamfered edge of the rod must face the crankshaft.

4 Install Piston Assembly

Insert piston, rings, and rod assembly number-1 into cylinder number-1 to start the cam-degreeing process. With a clean, white, lint-free shop towel soaked in engine oil, work the oil into the cylinder walls. Remember the cross-hatch pattern is designed to hold oil for sufficient lubrication. Also, be sure the tang is to the outside of the engine, the chamfered edge of the big end of the rod is facing the crank. Carefully install the band ring compressor and make sure the compressor rests on the deck surface. Compress the rings while making sure that they stay put in their ring lands. If one or more comes out, loosen the ring compressor and reorient the ring or rings on the piston and proceed.

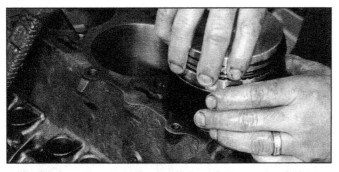

Work the piston into the piston ring compressor, which compresses the rings so that they are flush to the pistons. Once the piston and the rings have been properly placed in the compressor, push the piston into the cylinder using a non-marring tool, such as the handle of a soft-faced hammer. Do not force the piston in, but gently move it until it goes in the cylinder.

Make sure that the piston is properly oriented in the bore. Most pistons have arrows that point in a certain direction. Gently tap the piston into the cylinder until the piston is in the hole below the deck. At that point, put the hammer down, and use your hand to apply a smooth, pushing motion to the piston/rod assembly as it travels down the cylinder walls. Pay attention to how the piston feels during its travel. If there are any inconsistencies or disruptions in the travel, try to determine the cause of the uneven travel. Remove the piston slowly and examine it if there are any problems with the rings or cylinder wall.

5 Choose Cam Timing Gear

The Competition Products timing gear set and double roller chain should be considered by anyone interested in cam phasing. This crank sprocket provides nine keyways for nine different choices in cam timing: straight up; 2-, 4-, 6-, and 8-degrees advanced; and 2-, 4-, 6-, and 8-degrees retarded settings.

6 Install Cam Timing Gear

The cam timing gear comes as either the factory one-bolt or the heavier-duty three-bolt design (shown). Fasten the three bolts on the timing gear. To perform initial installation of the timing gears and timing chain, line up the timing marks on the gears and ensure that the chain is in the correct position. Lining up the timing marks on the gears is often referred to as installing the cam "straight up"; that is, neither advanced nor retarded. If the two gears were clocks, the timing mark on the cam gear would be positioned at the 6 o'clock point, while the crank gear timing mark would be at the 12 o'clock position. Make sure the chain has equal tension on both sides of the timing gear when installed.

7 Install Dial Indicator

Some people attach a piston stop across the piston to locate TDC. A dial indicator with a magnetic base installed over piston number-1 accomplishes the same thing with less chance of marking the piston.

8 Set Cam Timing

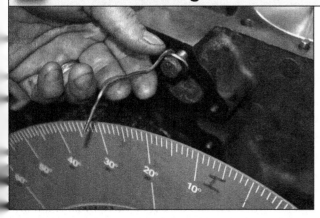

Create a pointer from a piece of coat-hanger-type wire. The wire is wrapped around the bolt sticking out of the water pump or timing cover holes, and bent as close to the degree wheel as possible in order to read the markings. Keep an eye on the dial indicator and turn the crank until you have the piston roughly at the piston's highest point. Line up the pointer with TDC on the degree wheel and "zero" the dial indicator.

Precision Measurement

8 | Set Cam Timing *CONTINUED*

Turn the crankshaft counterclockwise to .100 inch below the deck surface, and then rotate the crank clockwise until the dial indicator says that the piston is .050 down the bore. Record the reading on the degree wheel.

Continue to rotate the piston clockwise past TDC, until you arrive at .050 down the bore, and again record the reading on the degree wheel. If the crankshaft stopped at the same reading both before and after the TDC mark on the degree wheel, then the degree wheel is in the correct place. If the two readings were different, add them together and divide by two to get an average.

Loosen the degree wheel and adjust it until it reads that average number.

With the degree wheel in the proper place turn the crankshaft counterclockwise until you again pass TDC and arrive at .100 down, then rotate clockwise to .050, and check the number on the degree wheel.

Continue clockwise past TDC, to .050 on the dial indicator, and read the degree wheel again. The number should be the same. You have now arrived at true TDC. Turn the degree wheel to TDC, and zero the dial indicator.

Precision Measurement

9 | Check Piston-to-Deck Clearance

With the degree wheel at TDC, and the dial indicator at zero, slide the magnetic base to the outside edge of the piston, slightly lift the plunger so it clears the gap between the piston and the cylinder, and slide the base so the plunger lands on the deck surface. Slowly release the plunger and take the reading. If you do not have a dial indicator with the magnetic base, a straightedge across the piston and some feeler gauges also gives you the reading needed. Record the piston-to-deck clearance in your engine notebook. In the case of this engine that is being built to NHRA Stock Eliminator rules, the piston-to-deck clearance must be .014 inch.

Lobe Separation Angle (LSA): This is the spacing between the intake lobe and the exhaust lobe of the cam. The LSA is measured from the angle created by the centerlines of the lobes in relation to the camshaft itself, not to the crankshaft. The LSA must be balanced with other cam timing events, and therefore lift, duration, and lobe separation are critical timing events, and one definitely has an affect on another. Hence, a smaller LSA produces more torque at lower RPM,

and conversely, a wider LSA increases torque at higher RPM.

As a general rule, smaller LSA angles narrow the useable powerband, while larger LSA angles widen the powerband. In addition, larger LSA angles decrease compression, and therefore decrease the possibility of engine knock, while smaller LSA angles increase compression and the chance of engine knock.

Also, smaller LSAs reduce vacuum and often idle is inconsistent, but

larger LSAs typically offer increased vacuum and better idle characteristics.

Camshaft Degreeing

Verifying both the grind and installation of the camshaft is done through a simple procedure called degreeing the camshaft, which ensures that the cam is phased correctly with the crankshaft. In order for your engine to perform at its peak efficiency, every valve must open and

Though there are a few ways to degree a cam, the recommended method involves finding the intake centerline, which is the point where the intake valve arrives at maximum lift. If the installation were perfect, the cam, with a spec of 108-degree lobe in this engine ,would be installed straight up (neither advanced nor retarded) and it would have a 108-degree intake centerline.

Place some oil on the solid lifter (or the old hydraulic lifter that has been modified to stay rigid). Install the oiled lifter in the lifter bore of the intake lobe for piston number-1, which (in the B/RB engine family) is the second lifter bore from the front. Position the dial indicator so the plunger makes contact with the lifter. Rotate the crankshaft clockwise a few times and watch the lifter go up and down, making sure that the plunger remains in place and does not bind.

Zero the indicator with the lifter at its lowest point, which is referred to as the base circle of the cam. Continue turning the crankshaft clockwise and watch for the maximum lift on the indicator. Slowly continue turning the crank clockwise, watch as the lifter begins to rise, and then slowly stop turning when you arrive at maximum lift.

Turn the crank counterclockwise until the dial indicator reads .100 below maximum lift and stop.

Now turn the crank clockwise until you reach .050 below the maximum lift point, and record the reading on the degree wheel.

Continue turning the crank clockwise past the maximum lift, stop at .050 on its way down, and record the reading on the degree wheel.

Add those two readings from the degree wheel and divide by two. That number is the intake centerline.

My two readings added together and divided by two came to 110 degrees for my 108-degree camshaft. To correct that situation, the technician moved the crank sprocket from zero to 2 degrees advanced, resulting in a 108-degree position for the camshaft. The cam was now degreed in and confirmed as properly installed.

One note of caution: always take degree wheel readings while the crank is turning clockwise, which is its normal direction of rotation. This avoids erroneous readings caused by slack in the timing chain.

close at precise times in relation to the positions of your pistons. If the cam is out of phase with the crank, valves open early or late and severely hinder the engine's performance.

The standard practice for rebuilding an engine and installing a camshaft is to line up the dots on the timing gear set. After the cam has been installed, you line up the dot on the timing gear at the 6 o'clock position with the dot on the crankshaft gear at the 12 o'clock position. Many rebuilds, and even cam swaps for that matter, have been successfully accomplished without degreeing the cam. However, unless you take the time to degree the cam, the centerline of the cam cannot be known. Taking time to learn how to degree a cam provides the information and

assurance of a properly installed cam, or the need to correct an improperly installed or ground cam.

In addition to pointing out an installation error, degreeing the cam can confirm or deny that the camshaft is in fact the camshaft that is described on your cam card.

The very first step in degreeing a cam is to find top dead center (TDC). This is the place at which the piston has reached the highest point of its travel while the centerline of the connecting rod is parallel to the cylinder walls.

In order to find TDC, the short block must be assembled with the crankshaft, main caps, main bearings, camshaft, cam bearings, timing chain, gear set, piston/rings/rod assembly for cylinder number-1, and

the intake lifter for piston number-1. That intake lifter cannot be a standard hydraulic lifter, but must either be a solid lifter, or a hydraulic that has been modified to be completely rigid. With those parts in place, you fasten the degree wheel to the crankshaft snout complete with a crank turning attachment bolt that facilitates turning the crank either clockwise or counterclockwise.

As an example, the Comp Cams cam card for my engine (shown on page 106) indicates that the number-1 intake lifter at .050 inch off the base circle opens at 22 degrees before top dead center (BTDC) and then closes at 54 degrees after bottom dead center (ABDC).

The card also states that the duration for the cam "at .050" is 256

Comp Cams Cam Card			Jim Lewis Race Engines
Part Number: 23-000-6			Gring#: CRB3 5660/5662 H8
Serial Number: S 7599-10			SPC INSTR 1:
Engine			SPC INSTR 2:

Camshaft: CRB 3-bolt 383-440 Stocker
Part Number: 23-000-6
Serial Number: S 7599-10

Valve Adjustment	*Intake*	*Exhaust*
Gross Valve Lift	.432 inch	.432 inch
Duration at .006 Tappet Lift	302 degrees	310 degrees
Valve Timing at .050	Open	Closed
	22 BTDC, 54 ABDC	62 BBDC, 22 ATDC

Cam Installed at 106.0	*Intake*	*Center Line*
Duration at .050	256 degrees	264 degrees
Lobe Lift	.2880 inch	.2880 inch
Lobe Separation	108.0 inch	108.0 inch

The other specs are listed, and since the practice of degreeing a cam has been covered below, you should be able to confirm the information on your cam card. With your degree wheel still in place (and already confirmed to be accurately installed), turn the crank over a few times and get a feel for the intake lobe travel.

Make simple observations as to where the crank is in relation to TDC. Make sure the dial indicator is at zero as the intake lifter is on the base circle of the cam. When the lifter approaches TDC, slowly continue turning the crank until the indicator reads .050 and record the number on the degree wheel. (It should read 22 degrees BTDC, in my case.)

Resume turning the crank clockwise, go past TDC, noting that the lifter rises, peaks, and then begins to drop. Slowly bring the crank to a stop when it gets to .050 from the

degrees of crankshaft rotation on the intake lobe, and 264 degrees of crankshaft rotation on the exhaust lobe. Duration is typically measured when the lifter is .050 off the base circle of the opening side until it reaches .050 off the base circle on the closing side.

Degree the Cam

Important!

1 Orient Connecting Rod and Piston

The connecting rod and piston must be correctly oriented. Connecting rods have a chamfer on one side and are flat on the other. The side that is chamfered faces the crankshaft's rod journal fillet.

Precision Measurement, Torque Fasteners

2 Determine Main Bearing Clearances

Determining connecting rod bearing clearances is similar to the methods used to check the main bearing clearances. Working with one pair of pistons at a time, lay Plastigage on the bearing surfaces, torque the main caps to 85 ft-lbs (100 ft-lbs if you have ARP main cap bolts), and then remove the caps. The resulting crushed Plastigage is measured by the gauge on the wrapper to confirm correct connecting rod clearances. Caution: the connecting rods must be installed properly! The chamfered edges of the rods face the crankshaft fillets, while the flat sides of the rods face each other. Remember also that the rod bearing tangs must face the outside of the engine.

3 Measure Bearing Crush

If the crank moves while torquing the rod bolts, new Plastigage must be placed on the bearing surfaces, so be careful. If the crank does move, a small wood wedge may keep the crank from moving. The factory calls for connecting rod bearing clearance to be between .001 and .002 inch. Using the Plastigage wrapper, measure the width of the crush, and record it in your engine notebook. If your clearance is not within spec, you need to speak with your machinist to either find another rod or purchase undersized or oversized rod bearings.

base circle, and record the number on the degree wheel. (The number should be 54 degrees ABDC for our engine. You have now confirmed that the cam is installed correctly and that the cam seems to match the description of the cam card.)

The only way to truly know if the cam is completely and perfectly ground is to degree the cam at all 16 lobes. It may sound like a lot of work but every lobe should be inspected and confirmed that it was ground as the manufacturer claimed.

Rod Side Clearance

Remove all Plastigage residue and again torque the connecting rod caps to the rods on one pair of piston/rod assemblies. Measure the rod side clearance using a feeler gauge. The factory specification for the range of the rod-to-side clearance is .009 to .017 inch. It is important to have proper clearance between the pair of rods that ride on the same crankshaft journal.

After you record the first rod side clearance, move on to the next pair of pistons. Resist the temptation to only check the first pair of rods, and not the remaining six rods. As good as your machinist might be, an error could have been made on the machining of the crank, or the bearings could be defective, so check all eight connecting rod bearing clearances rather than risk catastrophic failure.

Rotating and Reciprocating Assemblies

Most of us know the sound of a washing machine that is in the spin mode, and then seems to take on a life of its own and begins rocking violently back and forth, banging against the walls and pipes. We know the terror of having to run down the stairs to stop that washing machine before it blows up and takes out the entire neighborhood! Having saved our families, we simply open the lid and move some of the heavy, wet clothes around, close the lid, restart the machine, and all is well. All citizens can return to their homes.

That washing machine's rotating assembly (going round and round) was out of balance, and you performed a balance job on the rotating assembly. In a similar fashion, if weight is not distributed evenly in your engine, you likely experience shake, vibrations, and certainly premature bearing wear producing bearing failure.

The crankshaft of your engine rotates and pistons move up and down. The big end of the connecting rod rotates, while the small end of the rod goes up and down. Some engine arrangements are inherently difficult to balance. Many V-6 engines incorporate balance shafts to produce a smooth-running engine. However, the good old American V-8, with cylinder banks at 90 degrees, is by design an easy arrangement to achieve balance. A V-8 has the luxury of piston movement where one piston's upward travel is balanced by another piston's downward travel.

The engine has a rotating assembly comprised of the crankshaft and the big end of the rod. It also has a reciprocating assembly, which is made up of the pistons, pins, rings, and the small end of the rod. Balancing an engine so it runs smoothly is a matter of making sure that the piston/rod assemblies all weigh the same, and that they offset the weight of one another. Further, the rotating assembly, which endures the stress of the reciprocating assembly, must be able to spin like a properly balanced washing machine.

So the first task is to determine the "bobweight," which is the total mass placed on the rod journal of the crankshaft. That number is arrived at by adding together the weight in grams of both big ends of the rod, both bearing sets in the two big ends of the rod, one piston and pin, one set of locks, one set of rings, and one small end of the rod. Additionally, about 4 grams are added for oil weight. The final step is to attach the bobweight to the crankshaft to simulate the total weight that the crank experiences while running.

Your major components should be balanced in order to rev through the entire RPM range smoothly without vibration. Though the reciprocating (up and down moving) parts like the small ends of the rods, the pins, pistons, and piston hardware have already been balanced during the connecting rod reconditioning, the crankshaft remains unbalanced. The journals of the crank have been cut .010/.020 inch, but again, final balancing is not performed until all pre-assembly work has been accomplished. That timing might be called preference, but it seems to make the most sense.

Final Pre-Assembly

Precision Measurement

1 Balance Crankshaft

Weigh all eight pistons with pins, and find the lightest piston/pin assembly. Weigh the pins separately to make sure they all weigh the same. If they do not weigh the same, modify the seven heavier pistons to bring them to the weight of the lightest one. Weigh the rods and find the lightest rod. Remove weight from the other seven heavy rods to make them the same as the lightest. Weigh the piston/pin/rod assembly along with one set of rod bearings, a pair of pin locks, and the rings for one piston. Calculate a bobweight and assemble and attach it to the crank.

Use a drill press positioned above the crank to take some material out of the crank, and test the crank again until it is perfectly balanced. You are now ready to begin final assembly, as all items have been checked, and the engine is balanced.

2 Install Crankshaft and Inspect Block Clearance

Squirt some assembly lube on the main bearing saddles. Install the crankshaft into the block and be very careful when lowering it into position so as to not damage the journals or anything else. Reinstall the main bearing caps and torque them to the required spec. Verify that the crankshaft turns easily and that there is no binding. The counterweights should not contact the block. The crank should be able to spin with little hand effort. If the crank does contact any part of the block, discuss the matter with your machinist and determine the best course of action.

FINAL ASSEMBLY

Building an engine properly means that components are installed and removed a number of times. If you have built a hot rod or two in your lifetime, you understand the difference of quality that exists between the hot rod that is mocked up and fitted prior to final assembly versus the

hot rod that was slapped together in a couple of weeks. In a similar vein, the engine must be mocked up by checking clearances, preparing parts for proper fitment, and testing parts to make sure they are correctly sized and fitted for the engine. Now that you have properly taken the time to

pre-assemble your engine, it is time to prepare for final assembly.

Never leave anything undone when you get to this stage. In other words, if there is some part that needs cleaning, painting, or even some machining work that has been ignored, now is the time to get it done. Avoid frustration by having everything ready to go.

Tools and Equipment

Think of the beginning of final assembly as preparing to perform surgery. All your tools should be clean and free of any grease or grime. Now is as good a time as any to perform a quick inventory of your tools, making sure that you have not only your specialized tools for assembly, but your basic hand tools. Are all your sockets handy? Do you have your calipers, dial indicators, and feeler gauges available? Are they clean and ready to use?

If you have a clean workbench, or even a heavy-duty table, it's always a good idea to lay out the parts that are

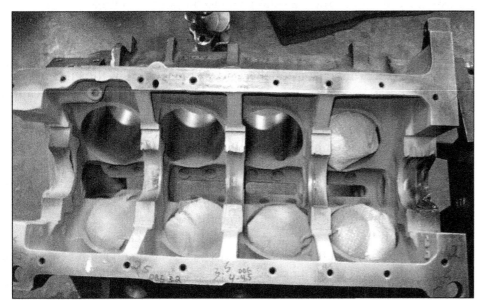

After trying different paints, we chose Ace Hardware Rust Stop. The Ace gray primer is first applied in interior areas that will be hidden as the engine assembly process progresses. It is best to mask off the lifter bores and deck surfaces. Any overspray is quickly cleaned up with lacquer thinner.

going into the engine and organize them in the order of installation. Not only are you better able to think about the various stages of the engine assembly, laying out the parts in one area is an excellent way to take a final inventory of parts and components necessary to get your engine running. Are all the gaskets purchased? Bolts and fasteners ready? Is the carburetor ready to be bolted on, or have you saved that rebuild until the end? Did you remember to buy the oil filter?

Taking Notes

One of the most common mistakes in building an engine is not writing down critical measurements and information that were gathered

Any surfaces receiving gasket material must be completely paint free. Again, thinner cleans those surfaces and creates a very sanitary, finished look to the engine. Here the end result of the paint work shows the block ready for assembly. All contact surfaces are clean, and the Jim Lewis signature red interior walls make for a very clean look, especially for helping you see the components being installed. They certainly make this block more photogenic!

during the process. Make sure to write down all pertinent information for your records. Even though it might seem a bit tedious, clearances, torque settings, and assembly notes can be extremely helpful after the engine is together.

Assembly Lube or Motor Oil?

Though there are standard methods in building an engine, a number of areas where one engine builder has his tried-and-true methods and practices can differ from another builder. For example, some builders are very committed to using assembly lube on the majority of parts that go into the engine, whereas another builder is more inclined to use motor oil for assembly. Two of my most reliable sources for engine expertise both rely heavily on standard motor oil for main bearings, crank installation, connecting rod bearings, and even camshaft bearings and lobes.

The use of motor oil as opposed to assembly lube on the camshaft might come as a surprise to some builders, but it must be noted that the Smith Machine lifters with the ceramic puck on the bottom of the lifter eliminates the need for cam break-in. For example, some builders might suggest motor oil on the cam bearings and assembly lube on the camshaft lobes. Another builder makes the point that all those components have to live on motor oil for its entire life, so why not use motor oil for assembly?

As an aside, do you have a catch tray underneath your engine stand? If you don't, you need to either purchase one that fits your engine stand or come up with a makeshift pan to fit under the engine because motor oil, solvent, and thinner comes off

the engine as it is assembled. Cleaning up the floor constantly during assembly gets old in a hurry, so spend a couple minutes to rig up a catch tray.

Painting the Inside of the Block

Painting the outside of an engine after rebuild is standard. Painting the inside of the block is more a matter of preference. Some do not paint the inside simply because it is too time consuming, or they fear paint breaking loose from those inner walls and clogging an oil passage, or worse. That said, there are some genuine benefits to painting the inside of the block. A painted surface speeds oil return, which is very desirable for an engine regularly in the 7,000-rpm range. The process calls for masking the block to avoid spraying the cylinder walls or saddles. Any overspray is immediately removed with thinner, resulting in a simple and effective process that is accomplished in stages.

Camshaft Installation

The next step in the final engine assembly process calls for the camshaft to be installed in the cam tunnel. Because of the requirement for assembly lube to accompany the camshaft installation, this job can be messy—a little forethought can make the job much less of a mess than you might expect.

When the cam was installed in this particular engine, Jim Lewis used Isky RevLube Assembly Lube on the lobes and Comp Cams Engine Assembly Lube on the journals. This lube was also applied to the cam bearings because it has a white lithium base, which provides excellent lubrication to both the cam journals and cam bearings. Get a recommendation for your particular camshaft from the manufacturer.

To decrease the mess, spread the assembly lube on the first and second cam journal and first four lobes. Once properly lubricated, insert the cam into the second journal and make sure the cam is able to turn freely. If there is any problem, stop the installation and investigate.

If cam installation is going correctly, lube the next four lobes and third journal.

Slide the camshaft in the cam tunnel and stop when the third journal enters the block. Lube the next four lobes and journal.

Continue the process until the cam is installed.

Once the camshaft is installed, reach into the engine to see if it turns smoothly. A cam handle is nice tool for both installation and for checking to see how freely the cam rotates. Any snags or disruptions in the cam means that the cam must be removed and the cam bearings checked for problems. You might have to take the block back to the machine shop if the cam bearings were installed incorrectly.

If the cam checks out, assemble the rotating and reciprocating assemblies of the engine.

Camshaft Installation

1 Remove Oil Drive Bushing

Before you install the new oil pump drive bushing in the block, remove the original bushing. This task was saved until now because the old OEM bushing conveniently serves as a shield from the paint work on the inner walls of the block. Use a screwdriver to pry the old bushing out. To install the new bushing, insert the oil pump drive bushing installation tool through the distributor shaft passage and line it up in the hole. When it is lined up, press it in with the installation tool.

2 Install Oil Drive Bushing

A couple of gentle taps on the installation tool helps get the bushing lined up in the hole. Instead of hammering the bushing into place, use a wrench on the installation tool to press the bushing into place. When the mating surface of the bushing meets the mating surface of the block, remove the tool.

3 Install Oil Galley Plugs

Install the oil galley and coolant passage drain plugs. A hammer and punch or appropriately sized socket can be used to seat the plugs. Make sure you don't miss any plugs in the bellhousing area. All the holes must be clear of debris. Use a thin layer of sealer on the threads to ensure a tight seal. In your engine notebook, make notes of the locations of these plugs. Further, do a quick diagram of the path of the oil and coolant, as this is the best time to see it, when the block is clean and empty. Tighten the plugs, being careful to not sink them too far in the block. Wipe off any excess sealer for a clean look.

4 Install Camshaft

The camshaft can now be inserted into the block. Use a cam installation tool to ease installation and avoid damaging the cam. Be careful as you guide the cam through the tunnel; you do not want to damage your new cam bearings or nick any of the cam lobes. To make the installation less messy, use the same method as when you applied assembly lube in stages when the cam was installed: cover the first journal, the first four lobes, and the next journal. Stop installing the cam, apply the assembly lube to the next four lobes and journal, and insert the cam up to that point. Continue in that fashion until the cam is completely installed.

Install Rear Main Seal

The rear main seal is necessary to maintain a leak-free seal around the rear of the crankshaft that protrudes from the engine. Clean the rear main seal groove of any dirt or residue from the old rear main seal.

1 Apply Silicone to Rear Main Seal

The rear main seal is necessary to maintain a leak-free seal around the rear of the crankshaft that protrudes from the engine. Use a brush and solvent to clean the rear main seal groove of any dirt or residue from the old rear main seal. Apply a thin bead of silicone to that groove.

2 Install Rear Main Seal

The seal has a lip on the top, which must face toward the front of the engine. The oil pressure pushes that lip outward, thus creating a continuous seal. If the rear seal is installed with that lip facing rearward, you will have an oil leak very soon after startup. Spread silicone evenly in the rear main seal groove. As you lay the seal in the groove, have one end sitting above the block so you can slide the seal into position flush with the block on both ends. This extra precaution helps ensure proper sealing.

When the rear main seal is correctly oriented and in place, the lip on the top faces toward the front of the engine. The crank sits in the groove in the saddle next to the rear main seal. Be sure to remove any sealer that has spilled into that groove. When the other half of the rear main seal has been installed, apply sealer on the parting line of the seal.

Install Cylinder Head Dowel

In order to perform machine work on the block, the cylinder head dowels located on the deck surface were removed. They must now be reinstalled. Obviously, the cylinder head dowel installation is necessary to perform prior to cylinder head installation. The dowels properly locate the cylinder heads. Prior to installing the dowels, make sure the dowel holes are clear of any gunk or debris.

During the machining process, the two cylinder head dowels were removed and now they must be reinstalled (if your machinist did not do it for you). Use a hammer to tap the dowels into place. Be sure to squarely tap on the dowel because if you miss it, you could damage the block itself. Place a piece of scrap metal next to the dowel hole to protect the top edge of the cylinder should the hammer miss the dowel. One miss with the hammer could create an unwanted gouge in the deck surface.

As oil travels down the valley, both the initial deburring and now the painted surface aid the oil flow and return. Inspect the deck for any dirt or foreign particles, then clean with thinner. Coat the cylinder walls with engine oil and rub it into the cylinders. Use a new, lint-free (oiled) shop towel to fully cover the lifter bores with oil.

Install Crank and Bearings

The main bearings and crankshaft have been measured for proper tolerances, and it is now time for final installation. Make sure to clean all components, and to have lubricating motor oil available to apply to all bearing surfaces. After torquing all caps to spec, the crankshaft should rotate freely.

1 Prepare Crankshaft for Installation

Though it may seem repetitive, give the crankshaft its final wash just prior to final installation. After you take the time to properly check all the clearances for the main bearings, the crank is ready to be installed.

2 Clean and Install Main Bearings

Using a lint-free shop towel, clean the main bearings and insert them on the main caps. With your fingers, press them into position. Main bearings have specific orientation for alignment so make sure to line up the tang with the notch in the main cap. If there is a specific upper and lower half of the main bearing, be sure each bearing is in the proper position. Install the caps without oil or lube, as they fit into the main cap with the tang mating to the notch in the cap. If you have any questions, refer to specific instructions from the main bearing manufacturer or consult a machinist. This is a critical step; be sure it's done correctly.

3 Lubricate Main Bearings

Spread engine oil on the main bearings prior to installation. Main cap number-3 is the thrust bearing, which is easily distinguished from the other bearings as it wraps around the sides of the cap.

4 Install Crankshaft

Apply a good coat of assembly lube and carefully lower the crankshaft onto the lubricated bearings on the main saddle. Make sure to lubricate the rear main seal as well. Install the crank keyway. Carefully and gently lower the crankshaft into the block. If the crank is too heavy for you, get a friend to help you lift it into the block.

5 Install Main Caps

Set the main caps into the correct position on the correct journals. The main caps are numbered 2, 3, 4, and 5 on the driver's side of the engine. The main cap without a number is the number-1 cap at the front of the engine.

6 Install Main Cap Bolts

If you are using stock OEM main cap bolts, torque the caps to 85 ft-lbs (in three progressive increments until the final torque spec is reached). ARP bolts are torqued to 100 ft-lbs, so be sure to hold the torque wrench properly and apply a smooth, steady pull during the entire process. Make sure the ARP main cap bolts turn freely and are all properly lubricated wherever

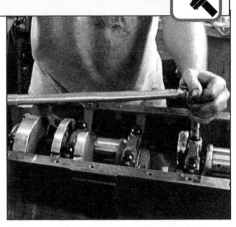

there is contact, in order to ensure proper torque readings.

We used Jim Hale's tried-and-true method for final installation of the crankshaft and main caps: Start with main cap number-3, which is of course, the thrust bearing. As you get the bolts started into the block, turn the crank about a half turn and make sure it spins freely. If all looks good, use your torque wrench to torque the cap to 35 ft-lbs, and then use a rubber mallet to hit the crank toward the front of the engine (as you did when you checked crank endplay). Turn the crank a half turn and make sure it still spins freely.

Begin the next torque sequence to 70 ft-lbs, and again strike the crank with a rubber mallet, and make sure the crank spins freely.

Finally, torque the main cap to 100 ft-lbs and turn the crank a half turn. Again, make sure the crank is not obstructed in its rotational movement.

After cap number-3 is installed, go through the same procedure and complete the main cap installation with number-5, -1, -4, and finally -2. Make sure the crankshaft spins freely without impediment. If the crank binds up, quickly pinpoint the location of the problem and evaluate whether the main cap, bearing, or crank itself needs attention. By the end of the installation, the crankshaft should spin nice and easy.

Precision Measurement

7 Measure Crankshaft Endplay

The engine should have a slight amount of front-to-rear crankshaft movement, which is required for normal operation. Use a dial indicator that is per-

fectly aligned with the crankshaft centerline. Using a large screwdriver, pry the crankshaft rearward and reset the dial indicator to zero. Then pry the crankshaft forward and note the amount of forward thrust displayed on the dial indicator. Factory specs allow for a tolerance of .002 to .007 inch. This particular 383 measures .007-inch crank endplay, which is within factory spec.

8 Lubricate Cylinders Walls and Bearings

Prior to final installation of the piston-and-rod assemblies, use a lint-free shop towel with engine oil to clean and lubricate all the cylinder walls. Then use

another shop towel to apply some engine oil to the piston skirts from the oil ring down. Of course, make sure there is assembly lube or engine oil on the crank journal and the rod bearing. Finally, put some oil on the ring compressor in order for the piston to smoothly move through it during piston assembly installation. Slip the rubber connecting rod bolt protectors over the rod bolts prior to installing the piston/rod assembly.

Critical Inspection

9 Inspect Rod Caps and Rod Bearings

Take some time to inspect the rod caps before installing the piston and rod assembly. If you removed the rod bearings from the caps for cleaning or inspection, do not just put them back on the rod. Make one last check of the connecting rod caps for any marks or burrs prior to installation. If you detect any irregularity, simply use a fine file to correct it. Once everything looks good, install the rod bearings onto the connecting rod.

Pistons and Piston Rings

Piston Rings properly fitted to a high-quality piston creates the proper environment for optimum efficiency in the cylinders. A number of jobs accomplished by the piston ring package are key factors in making the engine perform to its maximum potential.

First, the rings create a seal between the piston and the cylinder wall to keep combustion gases from escaping into the crankcase. Second, that seal helps create a stronger vacuum to draw in the fuel/air intake mixture. Third, piston rings scrape oil off the cylinder walls, which effectively results in aiding the cooling of the engine by using the oil to send heat from the cylinders to the block.

Our choice was a custom-designed ring package from Total Seal for the 383 Stock Eliminator engine going in my 1966 Coronet. That package includes a gapless top compression ring, a Napier-cut second ring, and a low-tension oil ring. The ring package used in this engine is intended for a specific drag racing application and the technology is quite remarkable.

The gapless top compression ring is a 1.2-mm multi-piece ring that incorporates a support rail that sends compression gas into the piston groove to push the ring out to the cylinder to create a better seal, and therefore better cylinder pressure. That rail closes the standard ring end gap, and minimizes blow-by, which is the escape of combustion gases past the rings into the crankcase,

resulting in a loss of power.

The second compression ring features technology based on the theory that the second "compression" ring is about 5 to 10 percent about compression control and 85 to 90 percent about oil control. Hence, the hook shape of the Napier-cut second ring helps remove oil from the cylinder walls. That feature allows the use of a low-tension third ring, commonly called the oil ring. Bottom line, the ring package is designed to minimize int ernal friction against the cylinder walls.

The goal of this engine is to build big power from mostly stock parts. Reaching that goal depends on our ability to build a short block that is not being hindered by power-robbing internal friction.

Install Piston Assembly

1 Place Piston in Cylinder Bore

Place protective sleeves on the connecting rod bolts to prevent damage to the crank journals and other components. Rotate the engine so the deck surface is horizontal. Make sure the pistons are properly labeled to go into the correct cylinder. Rotate the crankshaft so rod journal number-1 is at the bottom of its travel in relation to the block. Guide piston connecting rod assembly number-1 into the cylinder bore with one hand and hold the connecting rod with the other hand so it does not drag across the cylinder bore. Take your time to allow the piston to go down into the cylinder until the rings reach the top of the block. Rotate the rings so the end gaps are each at about 90 degrees from the next ring. In this orientation, the piston rings promote maximum cylinder sealing. Be sure to lubricate the ring pack with 30W oil. Make sure the piston wrist pins have enough lubricant on them before installing the pistons.

The piston/rings/rod assembly has the right parts. It's been pre-assembled to the correct specs, and now it must be installed properly. Before that assembly can go into the cylinder, piston and ring gap orientation must be determined. Proper ring gap locations in the piston at the time of installation are extremely important. Some people say that it does not matter since the piston rings rotate in the engine. Locate the rings so that they don't rotate past one another during break in. That condition causes a sizable leak in cylinder pressure.

How do you install the rings on the pistons of your B/RB big-block

2 Install Piston in Block

Carefully install the band ring compressor and make sure it rests on the deck surface. Compress the rings while making sure that they stay put in their ring lands. If one or more comes out, loosen the ring compressor and reorient the ring or rings on the piston and proceed. If the rings are not properly oriented, cylinder sealing and performance is adversely affected. Drive the piston into the cylinder using a non-marring tool, such as the handle of a soft-faced hammer. Once the ring pack has been placed well within the cylinder, set aside the piston ring compressor and drive the piston into the block with one hand while supporting the connecting rod from underneath the block with the other hand. Gently drive the piston into the cylinder until the connecting rod bearing firmly seats onto its respective crank journal.

3 Measure Crankshaft Journal

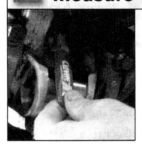

As the rod gets closer to the crank journal, guide it over the crank journal until it seats firmly on the journal. Remove the rubber protective sleeves and move the rod into position on the crank journal. Install the rod cap (with bearings installed) onto the connecting rod (OEM-style rod bolts must be torqued to 45 ft-lbs; ARP rod bolts, to 55 ft-lbs).

Once the piston rod assembly has been installed, make sure the crank turns freely. Continue to install the rest of the piston/rod assemblies in the block, checking rotation after every piston and verify that it is not binding, as well as being careful to avoid damaging the cylinder walls or crank journals. After you install the number-1 piston, install numbers-3, -5, and -7 in their cylinders and then piston assembly numbers-2, -4, -6, and -8 in their respective bores.

If you feel resistance during the piston assembly installation process, it could indicate a number of issues. For example, a ring is stuck in a valve relief notch or stuck at the top of the cylinder. Perhaps the ring gap is wrong or your ring compressor is too large or too small.

4 Install Connecting Rods

Remove the connecting rod bolt covers and install the connecting rod cap. Coat the bearing with assembly lube and correctly orient the cap to avoid backward installation. Using a specific moly-based lubricant recommended by ARP, coat the threads of the ARP bolts for use with the forged rods (here, RPM Internationals). Use the correct socket to tighten the nuts before moving on to the next cylinder for piston installation.

It will be harder to rotate the crankshaft as more connecting rods are attached to it. Insert a spare harmonic balancer bolt into the crankshaft snout and rotate the engine using a wrench. Obviously, with the pistons installed, it takes greater effort to turn over the crankshaft. You can check crankshaft rotational resistance after installing each piston assembly. A beam-type torque wrench is an excellent way to measure rotating resistance of the engine. If more than 5 ft-lbs of resistance is encountered after each piston assembly has been installed, some component has been incorrectly installed, the rings may not be correctly oriented in the bores, the rod bearings may not have the correct clearance, or they may not be adequately lubricated.

When all eight piston assemblies reside in the block and are fitted to the crank, rotating resistance should not exceed 40 ft-lbs.

Mopar? Let's say you are standing over the piston, looking down. Put the top ring end gap at 9 o'clock, the second ring gap at 3 o'clock, the top spacer for the oil ring at 9 o'clock, and the bottom spacer for the oil ring at 3 o'clock. As Jim Lewis puts it, "You want each ring to be 180 degrees from each other." As the piston is being pushed down the cylinder, remember to pay attention to any increase in the drag on the cylinder; it should go down fairly easy.

Take some time to inspect the rod caps before installing the piston and rod assembly. If you removed the rod bearings from the caps for cleaning or inspection, do not just thrown them back on the rod. Make one last check of the connecting rod caps for any marks or burrs prior to installation. If any irregularity is detected, simply use a fine file to correct it. Once everything looks good, install the rod bearings onto the connecting rod.

Various manufacturers have different recommendations for how to prepare the piston for break-in, so read the instructions provided by your piston ring manufacturer.

Prior to final installation of the piston and rod assembly, use a lint-free shop towel with motor oil to clean and lubricate all the cylinder walls.

Then use another shop towel to apply some motor oil to the piston skirts from the oil ring down. Of course, make sure there is assembly lube or motor oil on the crank journal and the rod bearing.

Put some oil on the ring compressor to allow the piston to move smoothly through it during the piston assembly installation.

Slip the rubber connecting rod bolt protectors over the rod bolts prior to installing the piston/rod assembly.

Rotate the engine so that the deck surface is horizontal. Make sure the pistons are properly labeled to go in the correct cylinder. Take your time to allow the piston to go down into the cylinder. Once the piston rings are in the cylinder, push the piston down the cylinder while watching and guarding the cylinder walls from undue damage.

As the rod gets closer to the crank journal, guide it over the crank journal until it's properly seated. Remove the rubber protective sleeves and begin to anticipate where the rod fits on the crankshaft journal. Move the rod into position on the crank journal, and install the rod cap (with bearings installed) onto the connecting rod.

Torque the bolts in three-step increments. (If OEM-style rod bolts are used, they must be torqued to 45 ft-lbs; ARP rod bolts must be torqued to 55 ft-lbs.) Once the piston rod assembly has been installed, turn the crank to make sure it turns freely.

Continue to install the rest of the piston/rod assemblies in the block, checking rotation after each piston and verifying that it is not binding. Also be careful to avoid damaging the cylinder walls or crank journals.

With the pistons and connecting rods installed, insert a feeler gauge between the rod and the crank filet. The factory-spec total clearance for two rods on one crank journal is .009 to .017 inch (which must be present as the two rods are moved from one side to the other).

As you look at the two connecting rods per crank journal, pry the rods forward to check rod side clearance. A large screwdriver is sufficient to pry the rods forward. When it checks to spec, pry the rods toward the back and check the side clearance of the other rod pairs.

All residue from the old seal must be cleaned from the rear main seal retainer. Use a small scraper and a knife, but be careful not to gouge or damage the retainer. Once the retainer is cleaned, make a final trip to the parts cleaner for a final scrub. Make sure the surfaces on the rear main seal retainer and the block are free of any contaminants.

Install the other half of the rear main seal in the retainer with sealer. Install the retainer with the bottom half of the rear main seal. Use a torque wrench and torque to 30 ft-lbs.

Install oil restrictors in the oiling holes on the deck to restrict the volume of oil that goes to the rockers. These holes are threaded during the machining process. Why use oil restrictors? In this race engine, the rockers receive enough oil. The desire is to send more oil to the main bearings. For a stock rebuild or a slightly modified street engine, you may not need extra lubrication to the main bearings, and therefore, oil restrictors are often not installed.

Install Gear Set and Degree Cam

The cam was already degreed during the preassembly, but because the engine came apart for final assembly, there is no escaping the necessity of degreeing it again. You can attempt to mark the timing gear and cam to recreate what took place during preassembly, but simply doing it again is the preferred method.

1 Install Timing Gear and Chain

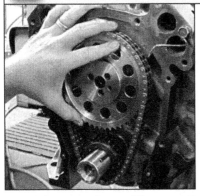

Put the timing gear in place with the timing chain, and line up the timing marks on the timing gear and the crank sprocket. Get the pointer ready for the degree wheel. Cover the camshaft with assembly lube for initial break-in procedures. Since my Smith Machine lifters have a special face to them, they do not require cam break-in.

2 Degree Camshaft

Set the engine up as described in the preassembly section, and Degree the cam to make sure that it is installed properly. Once you get the hang of degreeing a cam, it really is good reassurance that the engine is going together correctly.

Precision Measurement

3 Measure Camshaft Endplay

On a race engine, higher-RPM usage pushes the cam forward. In fact, the lobes of flat-tappet cams are cut on an angle in order to push the cam backward. If the cam moves forward, it advances the timing, something that could detrimental to the health and output of the engine. For that reason, a dial indicator is mounted to measure cam endplay. If endplay is more than spec, steps must be taken to limit it.

You must properly mount the dial indicator on the block. A minimal amount of camshaft movement front and back is typical. As you gently pry the cam forward, zero the dial indicator, the pry the cam backward. Pry it forward again, zero the dial indicator, and record the endplay in your engine notebook.

Camshaft endplay should be around .006 inch. If it is more than spec, check cam and timing gear installation. The fix is to install a plastic cam button on the front of the timing gear. Even if camshaft endplay is not a problem, most engine builders install this button as insurance to keep the cam from moving forward more than spec.

4 Install Timing Gear Set

Once the bottom end of the engine has been assembled, install the Competition Products timing gear set and chain. On my engine, I installed the smaller gear on the crank snout at the A2 mark, and then lined up the marks of the timing gears to the A2 mark, making sure that the chain was on the gears properly. I then tightened the ARP attachment bolts with a 3/8-inch socket and checked crank endplay to make sure that the crank was properly installed.

5 Remove Timing Cover Oil Seal

Use a hammer and a punch to remove the old front oil seal in the timing cover.

Use a seal driver tool to install the new front oil seal. The tool fits around the outside of the seal, and is tapped in with a hammer. However, a large pipe works as well, as long as you are able to maintain equal force around the entire seal. Put a thin layer of gasket sealer around the edges prior to installation.

6 Install Timing Cover

Place ample oil on the timing chain for initial startup. Be certain that the cover and block-mounting surfaces are clean and flat so a proper seal is attained. Smear a little assembly sealant on the gasket to hold it against the block surface. Fasten the timing cover to the block using ARP bolts torqued to 15 ft-lbs. Paint the cover engine color to make for a good-looking engine.

Dampener Installation

One procedure that demands close attention to detail is the installation of the harmonic balancer or some type of aftermarket dampener. I am installing an ATI Super Damper on my 383, and the dampener itself needs to be assembled before installation on the crank snout.

Unfortuatately, novices may first install the dampener on the crank snout and then assemble it. That is not a good idea. Damage to the keyway could result from that method. Rather, find a buddy who has a solid grip and have him hold it in place while you assemble the balancer as per instructions. Alternatively, you can position the balancer in a soft-jaw vise and complete the assembly of your dampener. Either way, always assemble the dampener prior to installation.

Don't throw the dampener on the engine without thinking. The impulse is often to grab a hammer and a block of wood and beat that dampener onto the crank. So here is a warning: Do not install the dampener, or harmonic balancer with a

The harmonic balancer, or in our case, the ATI Super Damper, prevents potentially damaging frequencies from traveling through the crankshaft. The dampener needs to perform exactly as designed, otherwise you risk engine failure. Get the proper harmonic balancer installation tool, and along with a very large crescent wrench, install the dampener/balancer properly.

An ARP center bolt requires a 12-point socket and must be torqued to 135 ft-lbs. The large spacer is also part of the ARP fastener. This bolt is stout and perfect for a street machine, but is heavy for a 7,000-rpm race engine. Therefore, the ARP center balancer bolt needs be replaced with the lighter OEM bolt for our application.

The addition of a windage tray calls for the use of two oil pan gaskets. The order of installation is engine, gasket, windage tray, gasket, oil pan. Make sure to clean the pickup, tube, and pan in the parts washer prior to installation.

hammer; there is too great a chance to damage the thrust bearing. Use the proper harmonic balancer installation tool and a very large crescent wrench to install the dampener/balancer properly.

If you think you don't need a balancer/dampener installation tool and use the center harmonic balancer bolt to press the dampener on the crank, you will very likely damage the threads on the crank snout. Again, beg, borrow, or steal (ok, don't steal) a proper harmonic balancer installation tool, and press the balancer/dampener on the crank just like the pros downtown. By the way, get ready for a nice workout when installing the dampener!

Oiling System

The B/RB big-block's lubrication system is adequate for street use in stock form. However, any high-performance driving, regular trips to the drag strip, or burnout contests require some basic modifications to the oiling system. For this engine build, the grooved main bearings in both the caps and the block saddles do much to keep the bottom end of the engine intact.

All B/RB (and Hemi) oil pumps are interchangeable. The B and RB engines use a 3/8-inch-diameter oil pickup tube, while the Hemi engines use a 1/2-inch pickup tube. Some racers looking for more oil volume incorporate a 1/2-inch pickup tube, but in this build, I elected to stay with the 3/8-inch tube. Since the Mopar Performance oil pan and windage tray are part of the oil system modifications (as well as the aforementioned chamfering of the oil passage holes), I increase oil flow to vital parts while using the stock pickup tube.

Oiling System Rebuild Tips

I had the privilege of spending some time with the Mopar drag racing legend Herb McCandless. Herb drove for the Sox and Martin Pro Stock team from 1970 to 1974. He later formed McCandless Performance and was very successful in supplying racers and enthusiasts with excellent information for building high-performance Mopar engines.

Herb gave me permission to include his tips on oiling systems for the B/RB and Hemi engines. Even though McCandless Performance is no longer in existence, the information is still valuable. Some of the information here describes work that needs to be done prior to building the engine, and some relates to where we are in the build of this 383 engine.

If you choose to perform these modifications Herb recommends that you precisely follow the procedure as described.

First, remove all five main caps. With a 9/32-inch drill bit that's 8 to 10 inches long, drill the oil passages from the top of the main saddle to the lifter galley on the passenger side of the block. Do not drill passages to the cam. Do not restrict the oil to the rockers.

Do not expect the windage tray to be perfectly flat. Spend some time flattening the contact area. Use a ball-peen hammer on a flat metal surface such as the top of your vise. Spend the time to tap and work the windage tray so it is flat. Use a straightedge to verify that it is flat. If it is not flat, an oil leak might result.

If you run a solid or roller lifter camshaft, cut off oil to the lifters on the driver's side of the block per the following instructions.

On the rear of the block, remove the pipe plug on the driver's side of the block next to the camshaft. Install a 19/32-inch freeze plug into the oil galley. Drive the plug into the block about 1¼ inches or until you can see the passage coming across the back of the block that feeds the oil to the driver-side galley.

Clean and install the pipe plug.

Oil is now cut off to the lifters on the driver's side of the block. The only way to cut off oil to the passenger side is by installing sleeves in each lifter bore.

On a street engine, McCandless highly recommends a Milodon #30930 pan and a street Hemi-size pickup (1/2-inch pipe). Re-drill and tap the block to 1/2-inch pipe. Even though there is a standard-size pickup available for this pan, a high-volume oil pump likes the increased volume of oil available to the pump. Once all

passages are drilled, completely clean the block very thoroughly. (A Milodon #34010 brush kit works very well.)

The only pan and pickup that McCandless recommends for race engines is the Milodon dual-line system. This has been the standard industry system for years. He does not recommend using a stock pan that has been deepened because this type of pan runs out of oil under acceleration and deceleration, which can cause spun bearings and broken rods—costly repair bills.

Oiling System Installation

1 Install Oil Pickup and Oil Pan

Mopar Performance offers a package deal of a stock 5-quart oil pan and a brand-new oil pickup and tube for about $100. The pickup screws in, and needs to be parallel with the bottom of the pan. Use a machinist's square to measure the distance from the bottom to the top of the pan. Check the measurement to the installed height of the pickup before you actually begin to install it, taking into account the two gaskets and the windage tray. You then have a rough idea of about where it will sit when installed.

2 Install Oil Pickup Tube

The oil pickup is threaded and screws in. Hold it with both hands to avoid bending the pipe. Once it has been positioned, it might need slight adjustment for optimal positioning.

Professional Mechanic Tip

PRO TIP

3 Measure Oil Pickup Area

Lay a straightedge over the pan rails to measure the distance from the approximate area that the pickup occupies, and record that measurement. IMPORTANT: You must also add the thickness of the oil pan gasket(s) and windage tray in order to arrive at the proper measurement. You can also use a square and adjust the height so you can see where the pickup is located.

4 Adjust Pickup Tube

If the pickup is not in the correct position, and turning the tube another 360 degrees does not solve the problem, use a small propane torch to heat the pickup tube. Once the tube has been heated, apply gentle minimal pressure to bend it into position. This job is not for gorillas, and be careful to avoid heating the pickup tube too much. Once it is in position, you need to verify that there is enough clearance between the oil pan and the pickup. The last thing you want is oil starvation on startup. Make sure there is 1/4 to 3/8 inch of clearance between the pickup tube and the bottom of the pan.

5 Measure Clearances

After recording the total depth of the oil pan, gaskets, and windage tray in your engine notebook, measure the height of the pickup from the oil pan mounting surface to the bottom of the oil pickup. It should be about 1/4 to 3/8 inch less than the pan's depth. Use a ruler to verify the clearance. Another method of measurement is to place a small piece of clay on the highest point of the oil pickup (keep the clay away from the pickup opening), install the oil pan, remove it, and measure the thickness of the compressed clay.

6 Paint the Block

A good plan is to paint the engine in stages as it is assembled. Spread some thinner on the block, wipe the area completely clean, and then allow the thinner to evaporate. Many builders assemble the entire long block, mask every hole and mating surface, and then paint the engine. You can either mask off the bottom end of the engine, or use a large piece of cardboard while applying paint to the block. One benefit of using the cardboard is that it is quicker, and there is no need to spend time looking for any residual adhesive from masking. Once the paint is applied, use thinner to clean off any overspray. Also the cardboard is a quick and effective way to paint the block while protecting the crank and rods.

7 Install Oil Pan

Apply a thin bead of silicone sealer to the oil pan mating surface. Then smooth out the bead with your finger. Cover the entire mating surface and take care to avoid applying too much sealant or you'll have a mess when the pan and baffle compress the gasket. Allow the sealer to set up according to instructions on the tube, and then lay the gasket down, making sure all the holes are lined up and able to accept the fasteners.

8 Clean Oil Pan and Windage Tray

Prior to installing the Mopar Performance oil pan and windage tray, make sure to do a final scrubbing of both parts. Installation of the MP pan and windage tray requires two oil pan gaskets, so have them on hand prior to installation.

9 Fit Windage Tray

Fitting the windage tray may need some slight taps from a hammer to flatten out some areas for optimum seal. Note the gasket between the windage tray and the block.

10 Install Oil Pan Gaskets

With the Mopar Performance windage tray in place, lay down a second gasket onto the mounting surface.

11 Apply Silicone to Oil Pan Gasket

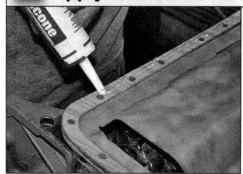

Apply silicone to both sides of the second gasket for proper seal. Then spread a thin bead evenly across the entire gasket.

12 Install Oil Pan

Finally, install the pan to seal the bottom end of the engine. Torque the ARP oil pan bolts to 15 ft-lbs. Tighten the bolts for the pan, one next to the other in order to maintain proper alignment.

13 Install ARP Fasteners and Assembly Lube

I used ARP's external fastener kit. Proper use of the ARP Ultra Torque Assembly Lube provides greater clamping force even if the ARP fasteners employ OEM torque settings. Tighten the pan in three stages for tight sealing of the pan, gaskets, and windage tray.

14 Clean Unpainted Areas

All unpainted areas need to be cleaned with lacquer thinner whether they are masked or not. As the block is painted, the oil pump mating surface is not painted directly, and again is cleaned with thinner after the paint has been applied. The mount for the oil filter is not the place you want paint overspray. Paint the external oil pump that beautiful Mopar Turquoise engine paint. I used a stock Melling standard pressure pump, and for our particular oiling system, the oil pressure from the stock oil pump was exactly what was needed.

15 Install Oil Filter Adapter

Attach the oil filter adapter to the oil pump, allowing you to install the Wix oil filter.

16 Install Oil Pump Drive Assembly

Install the Milodon steel oil pump drive assembly. The drive assembly runs off the cam gear and drives the oil pump. If you forget about this item, you will roast your newly rebuilt engine in a hurry. Make sure to apply a coating of assembly lube on the gear and the end that inserts into the oil pump.

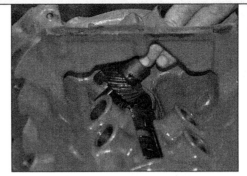

All B/RB big-block engines feature oil pumps that are driven by the camshaft through an intermediate shaft. The oil pump drive is inserted into the oil pump and meshes with the camshaft pump drive gear. Bolt the oil pump to the engine with a 9/16-inch ratchet wrench, and then torque to 35 ft-lbs.

17 Clean Cylinder Heads

To prepare the deck surface for the cylinder heads, apply thinner for absolute cleanliness to promote optimal adhesion of the head gaskets.

18 Install Head Gasket

Coat the Mr. Gasket head gaskets (PN 1135) with K&W Copper Coat. Allow to dry as per the instructions on the can. While drying, do a quick inspection of the cylinder heads to make sure there is no debris or foreign particles in any of the combustion chambers or ports.

With no other adhesive on the deck or the cylinder heads, position the Mr. Gasket head gasket. Be sure to follow the markings on the gasket that guide proper placement.

19 Thread In Head Bolts

Position the engine so that the deck is basically horizontal, and lay the cylinder head on the deck surface located by the two dowel pins. Once you are certain that the heads are correctly positioned on both dowel pins, gather the head bolts and prepare to install them.

Torque Fasteners

20 Torque Head Bolts

Torque the heads in proper sequence and to the correct spec. If you are using OEM bolts, they must be torqued to 70 ft-lbs; ARP head bolts must be torqued to 80 ft-lbs. As is the standard practice, tighten the bolts in three progressive steps.

21 Install Cylinder Head Bolts

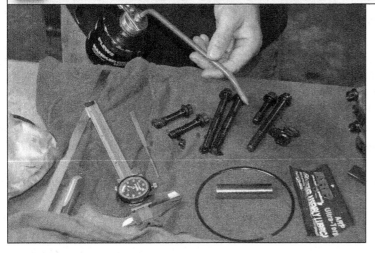

The head bolts on the Mopar big-block engine are not all the same length. Check with the pictures you took or your written notes concerning the cylinder head bolts and their orientation. If there's any question about their orientation, put the cylinder head on its side and trial fit the bolts until an equal number of threads are sticking out from the deck surface for each. Tighten the head bolts using the specific factory tightening sequence (see page 142) that's intended to evenly load the cylinder head and crush the gasket. Tighten the head bolts in three increments until you reach the final spec.

Valvetrain Geometry

The valvetrain is the sum of the lifters, pushrods, rocker arms, rocker shafts, rocker stands, valvesprings, valve retainers, valve locks, and valve seals. It is absolutely essential that all those components work together to accomplish one thing: to open and close their respective valve in as straight a line as possible. If the pushrod is moving up and down in anything less than a straight line, that movement introduces increased stress on parts, parasitic loss of power, and the possibility of premature wear or failure.

It has been mentioned earlier, but it bears repeating: The Mopar B/RB rocker shaft assembly in OEM configuration is a very good design, better than most other original equipment designs. For that reason, building a Mopar has the inherent advantage of solid engineering and performance capabilities. So whether you are using bone-stock valvetrain pieces or somewhat improved valvetrain parts, you are dealing with a great engine.

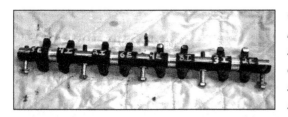

One of the great advantages of the Mopar B and RB engines for Stock Eliminator racing is the fact that the OEM design of the rocker arms is a shaft design that greatly adds to higher RPM stability. Rocker Arm Specialties takes stock rockers and rebuilds them with a high-strength steel shaft, and installs bushings in each rocker arm. The result is a strong, stable rocker arm system with the capability of 7,500-plus-rpm blasts.

Valvetrain Installation

Torque Fasteners

1 Fasten Rocker Arm Shaft

Refer to your notebook before attempting to install the rocker arm shaft assembly so you know how the bolts are arranged. Make sure all the proper retainers are in place. Using a 9/16-inch socket, tighten the rocker shaft snugly, then torque the bolts to 25 ft-lbs (see page 142 for the torque pattern to follow). The Rocker Arms Specialist shaft rocker system bolts to stock-height rocker stands and adds a major dose of security for high-RPM use.

2 Lube and Install Lifters

If you are using hydraulic lifters, soak them in engine oil for a few minutes prior to installation. When you remove the lifters from the oil container, be very careful not to drop them, as they will be slippery! Apply assembly lube to both ends of the lifters, and place them in the lifter bores. They should easily slip into position. Because these Smith Machine lifters feature a ceramic face, there is no break-in period as there would be for a standard lifter. That does not mean that the engine does not need break-in time, as the piston rings do need some break-in time.

3 Choose Pushrod Type

Comp Cams offers standard-length pushrods in various sizes as well as pushrods cut to your desired length. The custom units are especially helpful when dealing with higher-lift camshafts. By the way, I ordered a couple of extra pushrods to cover for any mistakes in measurements.

Professional Mechanic Tip

4 Determine Pushrod Length

If the pushrods are not the correct length, severe damage to the valvetrain can occur. To determine correct length, set a pushrod against the lobe of the cam where the valve is in the closed position. Set up a dial indicator on that corresponding valve retainer, and zero the indicator. Spin the engine a couple of times, zeroing the dial indicator until you can see that the valve is achieving full lift, as per your cam specs. If full lift is not achieved, calculate the amount of lift that is not being achieved, and add that amount to the total length necessary for your pushrod.

5 Determine Correct Pushrod Geometry

Prior to cutting all of your pushrods, create one in the size that you believe to be correct. The center of the tip of the pushrod must travel along the center of the rocker arm tip. Proper travel promotes valvetrain stability, especially at higher RPM ranges. Mark the tip of the pushrod with a Sharpie before you install it. Turn the crank over so you get rocker movement, and then remove the pushrod. Check the mark where the tip of the rocker made contact with the pushrod. The contact area should be in the middle of both the rocker tip and the pushrod tip. If that is the case, go ahead and cut the rest of the pushrods to that size.

6 Determine Pushrod Tip Length

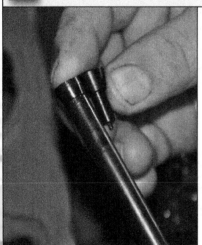

The length of the pushrod press-in tip must also be measured and added to the length of the pushrod itself to come up with the total length for your application. Do not include the length of the tip that inserts into the pushrod.

Don't be afraid to use cut-to-fit pushrods. Comp Cams offers stout pushrods that allow you to achieve optimum pushrod length. It is absolutely critical that the valvetrain geometry be correct for the build, and pushrod length must be correct. If the pushrod length is not where it needs to be, there will be certain binding and bent valves in short order.

Precision Measurement

7 Measure Pushrod Length

Pushrod length is a matter of evaluating your needs based on your cam specs and rocker arm assembly specs. For reference, understand that the stock length of pushrods for all B engines is 8.250 inches for a hydraulic lifter flat tappet cam, and 8.600 for a solid-lifter flat-tappet cam. If you are building an RB engine, the stock length of pushrods is 9.125 for a hydraulic-lifter flat-tappet cam, and 9.250 for a solid-lifter flat-tappet cam. These stock lengths are calculated for pushrods that are compatible with an adjustable rocker arm assembly. My particular engine requires a 9.300 pushrod, making the Comp Cams "cut to fit" pushrods the way to go.

8 Fit Valley Pan

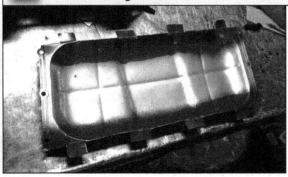

The OEM-style valley pan is designed to fit over the intake ports. In a stock grocery getter, this arrangement is not terrible, but in a performance application, the potential for flow disruption is immense. Trim the valley pan to retain it without relying on the intake manifold to hold it in place. Do not trim too much at a time, or you might need to purchase another valley pan (not the end of the world, as they are not very expensive). You can create a cardboard template as a guide to properly create your custom-fit valley pan. These edges have been sprayed blue to assist in seeing the embossed lines in the pan.

Install Intake Manifold

Many people probably never think much about whether there is a right or wrong way to install an intake manifold. In reality, there is more to it than slapping on a couple gaskets and dropping the intake in line with the bolt holes. You can save horsepower with a proper intake manifold installation, so take your time.

1 Clean Intake Surfaces

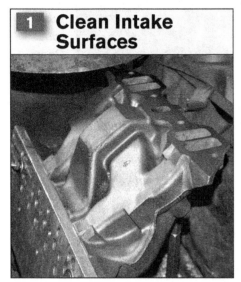

Prior to final installation, give the mating surfaces of the intake a resurfacing cleanup. The material removed from the intake might result in the need for a second intake manifold gasket, but no additional machine work on the cylinder heads is necessary.

2 Clean Intake

Scrub the intake to remove any leftover shavings or contaminants. Pay special attention to scrubbing and brushing the runners to make sure they are completely free of harmful particles.

3 Chase Carb Mounting Threads

Prior to final intake cleanup and painting, chase the threads that host the carburetor mounting studs. This factory cast-iron intake manifold was commonly found on 1968 and 1969 383 Mopars.

4 Align Intake Manifold

The first step in installing the intake manifold is to line up a straightedge with the top of the intake ports on the cylinder heads. Use a pencil or marker to draw the line created by the straightedge. Be sure the line is clearly visible.

Remove the straightedge and note the line created on the cylinder heads.

Line up the straightedge with the tops of the runners on the intake manifold. Again, use a pencil or marker to draw the line created by the straightedge. Again, be sure the line is clearly visible.

5 Fit Gaskets to Intake

Since both the heads and the intake have received a surface-cut cleanup at the machine shop, you probably need two gaskets for the intake, but begin with one gasket (per side). Use only a minimal dab of silicone to keep the gaskets in place.

Lay down the intake and line up the bolt holes. You want the lines that mark the top of the ports to line up with each other.

6 Match Intake Manifold to Heads

You may need to move the manifold slightly to match the lines created by the straightedge. You may discover that the one gasket is not thick enough to get the ports and runners to line up.

The quick remedy for the intake manifold not lining up with the heads is to add a second gasket. Again, use only a minimal amount of silicone. Make sure to get the port openings in the gaskets to match. Do not be surprised if the gaskets themselves have some slight variances in the port openings. Using a razor blade to clean up those openings in the gaskets takes care of it.

Mark the line from the cylinder head onto the gasket to make it easier to see the line on the tops of the ports. Verify that the lines match up. If they do, you just need to do a final cleanup, and give it a quick coat of paint before final installation.

7 Apply Silicone to Valley Pan

Run a bead of silicone around the mating surface of your custom-trimmed valley pan. Spread the silicone for uniform coverage.

8 Paint Valley Pan

Install the valley pan and press it onto the silicone.

Torque Fasteners

9 Torque Down Valley Pan

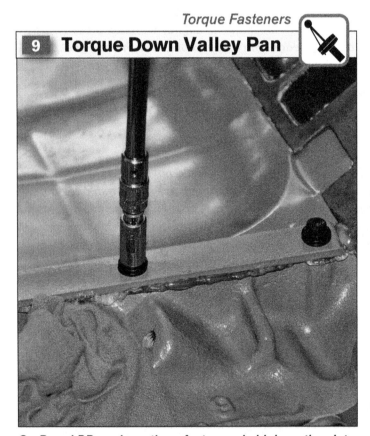

On B and RB engines, three fasteners hold down the plate on the front and rear of the valley. They keep the valley pan in place. Tighten the fasteners to 9 ft-lbs as per factory spec.

Important!

10 Seal Valley Pan

Do not skip this step! The valley pan is now held in place, but it needs to be sealed with silicone around the custom-made tabs. The silicone is up to the task of creating a leak-free seal, but take your time to seal all the edges of this pan.

11 Install Intake Manifold

After the silicone on the pan has dried, install the intake manifold. Spread the silicone on the gaskets, and use your finger to apply it to all surfaces, being careful to be neat so as not to reduce intake flow.

Lay down the manifold carefully, and remember to match up your lines on the tops of the ports with the tops of the runners. Make sure all the bolt holes line up, then press down on the manifold for a good seal, but do not disrupt the two gaskets per side.

Torque Fasteners

12 Torque Intake Bolts

Get the bolts started in all the holes, and then torque both the OEM or the ARP bolts to 40 ft-lbs using the factory sequence (see page 142). You are now looking at optimum flow from factory OEM equipment. Knowing that this manifold is sitting exactly where it should be is a confidence builder.

13 Install Pushrods

With the rockers loose, apply assembly lube to the pushrod tips. Move the rocker arm aside as you send the pushrods down to the lifters through the top of the head. Roll the pushrods around on the top of the lifter to spread the assembly lube, and then bring the pushrod in line under the rocker. Tighten the rocker for installation purposes only, as you will soon be adjusting the valves.

The long block has been fully assembled.

Final Installation and Adjustments

With the motor positioned on the dyno, and anticipation levels high for the first start up, the tendency is to throw theses external engine components on too hastily.

Be careful to have all instructions handy for suggestions from the manufacturer. Lay out all fasteners and clips to minimize mistakes. Be willing to back up, and redo instal-

lation on these brand-new components. A thin layer of motor oil on fasteners is suggested, as well as care to run the wires to proper locations.

Torque Fasteners

1 Install Starter

Bolt on the Powermaster mini starter and torque the starter bolts to 50 ft-lbs. Although there is no greater sound on the planet than the standard equipment Mopar starter, this Powermaster XS Torque starter provides 200 ft-lbs of cranking power, promises no heat-soak problems, and weighs 8.4 pounds.

2 Choose Carburetor

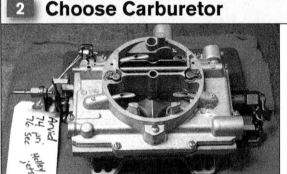

NHRA Stock Eliminator racing requires using the carburetor that originally came on the car. In stock form, the Carter AFB does not provide enough fuel and air to adequately feed the 383 race engine in the higher RPM ranges. This OEM Carter AFB 4131

carburetor was purchased on an eBay auction for $35. Dean Oliver, owner of Deano's Carburetors, did a fantastic job rebuilding this carburetor to better-than-new standards. Especially helpful on this AFB is the conversion that allows the use of standard Holley jets. Dean spent time making sure that the linkage ran smoothly, the carburetor experienced complete wide-open throttle, the gaskets fit perfectly, and all internal parts were exactly on spec.

3 Install Carb, Fuel Lines and Linkage

Place the carburetor gasket on the intake manifold, and install the carburetor. Lay the gasket on the intake manifold with no sealer, place the carburetor on top of the spacer, and install the carburetor studs and tighten with a 1/2-inch open-end wrench. With a pair of pliers, install fuel lines and the dyno throttle linkage with the common clip that attaches to the carburetor linkage.

4 Install Headers or Exhaust Manifolds

The ceramic coating on the Hooker Super Competition headers not only looks fantastic, it also helps decrease underhood heat. Use ARP header bolts

for installation. Many of you building engines to stock specifications are using your exhaust manifolds. However, the differences found in horsepower between headers and exhaust manifolds is significant. Exhaust manifolds are certainly more quiet than headers, and they maintain the originality of the vehicle. But the contention that headers don't fit well or that they are not practical for street operation seems unwarranted, especially if you opt for high-quality headers from a reputable vendor like Hooker. Free-flowing exhaust is a simple horsepower gain that usually results in better gas mileage, as well.

5 Install Water Pump

The Meziere Enterprises water pump is a simple bolt-on installation that produces leak-free operation without skipping a beat. Spending a little extra money on an electric water pump not only aids in cooling, it does not rob horsepower to run it.

6 Install Valve Covers

Install the Edelbrock valve covers even though they will be coming off again for valve lash adjustment. The valve cover gaskets sit nicely in the valve covers. Tighten the valve cover bolts with a 7/16-inch open-end wrench or a 7/16 thin-wall socket.

7 Prime Oil Pump

Use a drill and oil pump drive attachment to prime the oil pump and bring oil pressure to the lifters. Once the lifters are pumped up, valve lash can be set.

8 Adjust Pushrod

Once the engine has been rotated to the point that the exhaust valve for cylinder number-1 begins to open, you can adjust the intake valve on cylinder number-1. To adjust the pushrod down onto the lifter use the rockerarms.com shaft rocker arm assembly. As you adjust the pushrod down, spin it until it just begins to have some resistance as it contacts the lifter. Then lock down the adjustment in order to begin valve lash adjustment.

9 Adjust Valve Lash

Valve lash is simply the distance between the valve tip and the rocker arm tip. Since this 383 engine is using the Smith Machine (Schubeck-style) hydraulic lifters, the adjusting nut is loosened to allow a proper-size feeler gauge to be inserted between the valvestem and the tip of the rocker arm. The adjusting nut is then tightened down, and the valve lash adjustment is complete.

9 | Adjust Valve Lash CONTINUED

Many engine builders differ on the techniques and settings for valve lash adjustment. While we started with .002 valve lash on both intake and exhaust, it is likely that we might increase that number to see if it helps performance.

Opinions on valve lash settings vary, so to some degree you have to be willing to experiment in order to achieve the maximum performance from your engine. Having a fast and competitive race car depends on your willingness to flog your car. Experiment with valve lash; try different combinations of engine setups. If you've got the time, you can arrive at the level of performance that gives you an edge on race day.

10 | Distributor

Whether you are rebuilding a high-performance street engine or a race engine, an upgrade to the distributor is well worth the investment. Not only is the spark going to be stronger, but you have greater reliability with a quality distributor as from MSD. To install the distributor, bring piston number-1 to TDC on the compression stroke. Line up the rotor tip with the number-1 piston terminal and drop the distributor into place. Install the distributor hold-down clamp using a 9/16-inch ratchet wrench. The firing order of the Mopar B/RB engines is 1-8-4-3-6-5-7-2, and the distributor spins counterclockwise. As you install the wires, make sure the ignition wire is installed on the correct spark plug for the particular cylinder.

Line up and install the distributor, making sure to check firing order so that the distributor is lined up properly.

DYNO TESTING RESULTS

The moment of reckoning has arrived. The engine must be properly installed on the dynometer, and prepped for first startup. High-quality components are installed, proper break-in oil is ready, valve lash has been adjusted, and all wires must be checked. If it is at all possible, I highly recommend that you have your engine builder run the motor on the dyno to make sure that there is no major problem in engine assembly. Further, if the motor is being built for high-performance application, make sure your money was well spent in all those expensive services that were supposed to add torque and horsepower. Last, hearing that motor fire for the first time is always exciting and extremely rewarding for all the time and effort spent in making things right.

Our long block engine was brought into the dyno room at Jim Lewis Race Engines to work toward setup for some dyno pulls to gather horsepower and torque numbers. Since the engine sits up higher on the dyno than on an engine stand, finishing the assembly of the engine's external parts while on the dyno is much easier. Although accessibility makes installation simple, care is taken to make sure that fasteners are properly torqued and that components fit well.

Setting Valve Lash

Adjusting the valves and creating proper valve geometry is a science in itself. Most stock big-block Mopars are equipped with stamped rocker arms that are not adjustable. If you are using them, setting the valve lash depends on either pushrod length, shortening the tips of the valves, or putting shims under the rocker shaft to work with your particular combination. Many engine builders recommend focusing on getting the proper

Excitement is building as the engine is rolled into the dyno room for final assembly of external components. The engine must be installed to the dynonometer for initial startup and testing.

pushrod length, and letting the lifters settle in during break-in.

If you have adjustable rocker arms, you must set the valve lash prior to start-up. (Valve lash is the clearance between the rocker arm tip and the valvestem tip.) The process might be considered complicated, but it is actually quite simple, though just a bit a tedious. Note: There are differences in procedure for setting valve lash for standard hydraulic, Smith Machine, and solid lifters.

Stock Hydraulic Lifters

At this stage in an engine rebuild, the rocker shaft assembly has already been installed. And although lube should have been applied at installation, double-check to make sure there is a dab of Comp Cams or comparable assembly lube on the tips of the rockers and the valvestems.

To Set Valve Lash for the Intake Valves: Using a drill with an oil pump driver attachment, spin the oil pump to produce oil pressure to pump up the hydraulic lifters. Starting with cylinder number-1 (the second valve from the front of the engine), turn the engine over in its normal clockwise rotation with a wrench at the ATI Super Damper bolt. Watch for when the exhaust valve just begins to open. At that point, adjust intake valve number-1 by loosening the adjusting nut while you spin the pushrod until you feel free play in the rocker arm.

Tighten the adjusting nut while simultaneously spinning the pushrod with your fingers. You will soon feel resistance in the spinning pushrod. That is "zero lash" (no clearance between the pushrod and the rocker).

Turn the adjusting nut 1/2 turn farther. That extra 1/2 turn establishes the correct preload for the rocker arm, pushrod, and lifter.

Follow the firing order of the engine, turn the crank, and follow the same procedure of setting the intake valve lash for the other seven cylinders.

To acomplish this, go back to cylinder number-1 and turn the engine over until the pushrod for intake valve number-1 begins its travel. Immediately after maximum lift, the intake valve begins to close. At that point, stop turning the engine over. If you continue to turn the engine past about halfway, the exhaust valve begins to open and you turn the engine over until you can start again with cylinder number-1.

To Set Valve Lash for the Exhaust Valves: Similar to the procedure for setting lash for the intake valves, tighten the exhaust valve adjusting nut until you begin to feel slight pressure against the pushrod. You are at zero lash for the exhaust valve. Turn the adjusting nut another 1/2 turn, and you are done.

Follow the firing order of the engine, and go through the same procedure with the other seven cylinders.

Smith Machine Lifters

Setting valve lash (for intake and exhaust valves) with Smith Machine lifters is similar to setting it with standard hydraulic lifters with one exception: Rather than turning the adjustment nut 1/2 turn after zero lash, you simply insert the recommended-size feeler gauge between the tip of the valvestem and the rocker arm tip (.002 inch in our case).

Tighten the adjusting nut, and adjust the other seven cylinders accorded to the firing order.

Solid Lifters

You do not need to spin the oil pump since these lifters only require

oil pressure for lubrication. Make sure to read your cam card, or consult with your cam supplier for recommended valve lash specifications.

To Set Valve Lash for the Intake Valves: First, you must place the lifter on the base circle of the camshaft. Using the wrench on the harmonic balancer bolt, turn the engine until the intake valve for cylinder number-1 begins to open.

Loosen the adjusting nut until you can feel that the rocker arm is slightly loose. Insert the proper-thickness feeler gauge between the valvestem tip and the rocker arm tip and tighten the adjusting nut until the feeler gauge has some resistance as you pull it out. Pull the feeler gauge out completely and tighten the adjusting nut.

Work through the firing order of the engine to complete the other seven intake valves.

To Set Valve Lash for the Exhaust Valves: Turn the engine over until the exhaust valve of cylinder number-1 opens to maximum lift, and then begins to close.

Loosen the adjusting nut on the rocker, and insert the recommended-size feeler gauge between the valvestem tip and the rocker tip. Tighten the adjusting nut until the feeler gauge faces some resistance as you pull it out. Pull out the feeler gauge completely and tighten the adjusting nut.

Work through the firing order of the engine to complete the other seven exhaust valves

Note: When Comp Cams gives valve lash setting for solid lifter cams, they are "hot" settings. Since the engine prior to break-in is cold, you need to do the initial start up of your engine, and then adjust the valve lash a second time after shutting down your engine.

Break-In

When breaking in a stock engine, you would do well to purchase break-in oil from either Joe Gibbs or Brad Penn. Specifically intended for initial startup, these oils are enhanced with zinc and other chemicals that help to properly break in the camshaft and ultimately seat the piston rings.

First Dyno Pull

When everything was installed, all fluids added, all fasteners checked, and valve lash set, one of the employees fired up the engine. He immediately took it up to about 1,800 rpm, and made it hover from about 1,800 to 2,200 rpm until it reached operating temperature (about 15 to 20 minutes), and then shut it off off.

At the end of that initial startup, the cam was broken in. He next inspected to confirm that it was healthy.

He removed the valve covers, checked the valves, and looked for any telltale signs of trouble. Loose valves indicate a flattened cam or some valvetrain failure. Water in the oil gives the oil a milky appearance. Everything checked out well enough to put the valve covers back on the engine. The engine was allowed to cool down prior to beginning a second dyno pull.

Second Dyno Pull

After cool down, the employee started the engine again, and did an initial light pull, to 5,500 rpm. (Later pulls will likely go higher, but we are again confirming that the engine is in good shape, and able to take on further testing.) After the second pull, he checked the valves and looked for any trouble in the oil. All was well so the engine was tested at higher RPM ranges.

Additional Dyno Pulls

In the case of this 383 engine, the third through sixth pulls involved running the engine up to 6,800 rpm, and then shutting down, with a cooldown between each pull.

Between each run, Jim examined the valves, checked for leaks, and looked at the numbers on the graphs. After feeling confident about the engine, subsequent pulls were focused on tuning and performance enhancements.

It would have been nice to spend a week working on various combinations, but even the day spent at the dyno was profitable for evaluating what showed promise and what might not be helpful for making power. There is more testing to do, but hearing that engine fire up for the very first time was a great thrill. It is now time to get this 383 Stock Eliminator engine into my 1966 K/SA 1966 Coronet and go racing!

Dyno Test Procedures

The dyno at JLRE is equipped with an MSD 6A box for controlling spark to the engine. An MSD Blaster coil is also part of the dyno, and is quickly installed in preparation for start up.

1 Choose Engine Break-in Oil

Opinions on how to break in an engine vary. Some builders like to use oil that is specifically manufactured for break-in. Oils like the Joe Gibbs Break In Oil, or the Brad Penn Break In oil are currently widely used. Both those contain high concentrations of zinc and other ingredients, which promotes proper break-in for both camshaft and piston rings. Check with your engine builder as to his preferences. Speaking of oil, a Wix racing filter is definitely the filter of choice for our application. Make sure your oil filter is capable of staying together if you intend to do any high-performance driving.

2 Add Gas

With all external parts installed, the engine was ready to fire. Everett poured the 110-octane racing gas into the dyno room's fuel cell.

3 Perform Final Checks

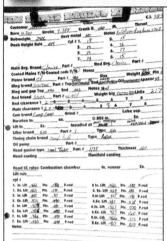

A quick look at the summary sheet for the engine served is a reminder of all the work that had been done to the engine. Bearing clearances had been checked, valve to piston clearances had been confirmed, lift numbers were measured, and deck height was recorded all within NHRA rules for the 383 engine.

4 Start Engine

Jim Lewis gets situated at the console while Everett makes a final check of all connections and engine

components. When everything looks ready, Jim hits the starter button, and the engine immediately fires to life.

5 Run Engine

Hearing this engine run for the first time was a definite thrill. It sounded nasty. In fact, a number of the locals came to the shop to catch

a glimpse of what was going on. For initial start up, Jim ran the engine for about 10 minutes at the 1,800-rpm range, varying the RPM slightly during that time. This initial start-up procedure is necessary to properly seat the piston rings and give the valvesprings a proper heat set.

6 Inspect for Trouble

Jim immediately removed a spark plug to determine combustion. Everett was hovering around the engine, checking all fasteners and inspecting for any

leaks or obvious problems. After everything checked out fine, the engine was allowed to cool down, and then it was fired up again. The second pull was a trip into higher RPM territory—about 5,500 rpm. The engine was shut off, numbers were examined, vitals were checked, and the engine was again allowed to cool. After cool down, the engine was fired up to 6,800 rpm. It sounded healthy and did not skip a beat throughout the RPM range.

7 Change Carb Jetting

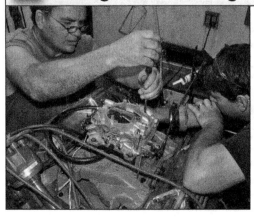

After a couple more pulls up to 6,800 rpm, Jim decided to experiment on the carburetor jetting to see if he could gain some power.

8 Inspect Carb

The Deano Carburetor came apart effortlessly and was as spotless on the inside as it was on the outside.

9 Replace Jets

Not a bad carburetor for $35, right? The interior is spotless, encouraging tuning and experimentation with jet sizes. The jets simply unscrew and install with a screwdriver. Jim replaced the number-74 and -76 jets with smaller -73 and -75 jets.

10 Change Oil

One of the experiments on the dyno included changing to Mobil 1 Synthetic 5W-20 oil. The oil showed a benefit at some points in the power-band, but a loss in power in other, lower RPM ranges.

11 Choose Headers

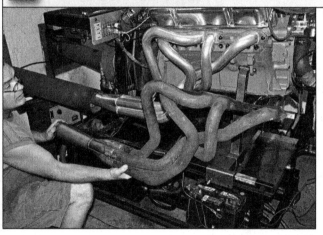

Like any good engine builder, Jim Lewis has headers on hand for most of the popular engine combinations, including a set of identical Hooker Headers for my 383 engine. Please note that my headers (installed, left) are far better look-ing than Jim's headers (in his hands, left), but his headers have Performance Welding Merge Collectors installed. The Perfor-mance Welding Merge Collectors (above) make power by main-taining the speed of the exhaust gases throughout the length of the header and collector. The result is that the headers become more efficient in scavenging the exhaust gases from the engine. Performance Welding builds merge collectors for each particular engine and race car combination. The result is improved horsepower and torque.

12 Change Jetting Back

Jim concluded that he needed to go back to the original jetting in the carburetor. The number-73 and -75 jets were removed and the original, bigger, number-74 and -76 jets were re-installed.

Dyno Testing

Prep for initial startup included using the drill with oil primer attachment, and priming the oil pump, and getting Valvoline 10W-30 Racing Oil up to the heads. Timing was set at 42 degrees, fuel pump turned on, and the Powermaster starter was engaged. The engine fired up immediately; I didn't even hear the starter. But I did hear the engine, and it sounded like 1,000 hp. The initial ten minutes of running had the engine at about 1,800 rpm. (The Smith Machine lifters do not require any break-in time, as they ride on the ceramic pucks.) Everett stayed by the engine, checking for leaks, until it was time to make the first pull. When the engine was warmed up, Jim did an initial pull of 6,800 rpm, and then shut off the engine to adjust valve lash.

Results

The initial start up was a matter of seating the rings, so there was no dyno pull with numbers. In other words, Test 1 was the third time the engine had been running. After Test 1, there were about three or four subsequent pulls without any changes to the engine. During those pulls, Jim ran the engine up to 6,800 rpm, and evaluated horsepower and torque numbers, fuel curve, and combustion as evidenced by residue on the spark plugs. All vitals were checked, including engine temperature, oil temperature, and oil pressure.

The first change made to the engine's original tune was to change the jets in the carburetor, then perform Test 2. The smaller jets actually decreased the power.

Test 3 involved a swap to Mobil 1 5W-20, bringing about some increased power above 6,000 rpm, but under 6,000 rpm, the Mobil 1 resulted in less power than the Valvoline oil.

Test 4 involved changing the Hooker Headers to Hooker Headers that had been modified to accept Performance Welding Collectors, and there was definitely some power gained as a result of the merge collectors.

The final test, Test 5, included a swap back to the bigger jets, which improved power as well.

Test Summary

Test 1: Initial start up, Carter AFB with jets number-74 and -76, Accel 123 Spark Plugs, valve lash at .002, timing at 42 degrees, Valvoline 10W-30 Racing Oil, Hooker Headers (without merge collectors)

Test 2: Change Carter AFB Jets to numbers-73 and -75

Test 3: Change to Mobil 1 5W-20

Test 4: Replace standard Hooker Headers Super Competition Headers with Hooker Super Competition Headers with Performance Welding Merge Collectors

Test 5: Changer Carter AFB Jets to numbers-74 and -76 (as originally equipped at start up)

The final two dyno pulls were performed with the Performance Welding Collectors, the number-74 and -76 jets, 42 degrees timing, Mobil 1 synthetic oil, and valve lash still at .002. Best numbers for the final pull of the day produced 446.4 ft-lbs of torque at 4,100 rpm and 431.8 hp at 5,500 rpm.

Mission accomplished, the engine is taken off the dyno, tidied up a bit and adorned with an Edelbrock air cleaner that compliments the Edelbrock valve covers. Although the rebuild of this engine was a challenge, it was also a very rewarding learning experience.

Dynometer Test Results

After we assembled the engine, we performed the initial leak checks, ensured that the engine was running up to standards, and broke in the engine. Once these procedures had been performed, we installed the engine on the dyno to see the results of our work. The dyno runs confirmed that we had a strong-running Chrysler B engine that would be suitable for competition.

RPM	Test 1 Torque	HP	Test 2 Torque	HP	Test 3 Torque	HP	Test 4 Torque	HP	Test 5 Torque	HP
4100	**452.1**	352.9	**453.4**	353.9	**459.5**	350.0	445.3	347.6	**446.4**	348.5
4200	449.3	359.3	451.7	361.2	452.2	361.6	446.8	357.3	445.7	356.4
4300	448.1	366.9	450.7	369.0	449.2	367.8	449.9	368.4	443.5	363.1
4400	444.8	372.7	445.9	373.6	445.4	373.1	443.6	371.6	442.0	370.3
4500	442.4	379.0	446.2	382.3	446.2	382.3	439.7	376.8	440.1	377.0
4600	440.3	385.7	446.1	390.7	**443.9**	388.8	**443.9**	388.8	438.5	384.1
4700	440.4	394.1	434.3	388.6	437.4	391.4	437.0	391.1	433.2	387.7
4800	435.5	398.0	434.4	397.0	438.7	400.9	434.4	397.0	433.8	396.5
4900	435.2	406.0	434.7	405.5	434.7	405.5	435.0	405.8	431.3	402.4
5000	434.3	413.5	429.9	409.2	432.2	411.5	431.3	410.6	429.6	408.9
5100	430.0	417.5	432.0	419.4	429.1	416.7	425.3	413.0	427.3	414.9
5200	425.9	421.7	426.1	421.9	428.4	424.2	423.6	419.4	426.6	422.4
5300	417.1	420.9	424.4	428.3	421.8	425.7	422.5	426.3	419.0	422.8
5400	409.3	420.8	418.8	430.5	416.4	428.2	414.4	426.1	415.9	427.6
5500	401.0	420.0	409.5	428.9	408.6	427.9	408.7	428.0	412.4	**431.8**
5600	398.5	425.0	404.7	431.5	401.7	428.3	397.9	424.3	401.1	427.7
5700	390.7	424.0	400.9	435.1	395.7	429.5	396.2	430.0	395.5	429.2
5800	385.7	**425.9**	395.4	**436.6**	387.3	427.7	391.8	**432.7**	389.9	430.5
5900	374.5	420.7	384.3	431.7	379.7	426.5	380.6	427.5	375.2	421.5
6000	367.8	420.1	369.9	422.6	376.4	430.0	370.1	422.8	363.7	415.5
6100	363.7	422.4	365.0	424.0	370.7	**430.6**	364.8	423.7	355.7	413.1
6200	359.1	423.9	359.2	424.0	359.5	424.4	361.5	426.7	351.7	415.1
6300	351.4	421.5	352.6	423.0	349.8	419.6	356.4	427.5	344.6	413.3
6400	343.4	418.4	346.3	422.0	345.4	420.9	345.9	421.5	345.4	420.9
6500	339.1	419.7	342.5	423.9	339.6	420.3	339.3	419.9	338.9	419.4
6600	328.4	412.7	337.2	423.8	327.9	412.1	336.5	422.9	325.3	408.7
6700	320.2	408.5	334.7	427.0	316.4	403.6	323.0	412.0	320.7	409.1
6800	308.4	399.3	316.0	409.1	312.4	404.4	311.8	403.7	311.3	403.1

TORQUE SPECIFICATIONS FOR FASTENERS

Intake Manifold Torque Sequence

This is the correct torque sequence for the intake manifold. Final torque specification is 40 ft-lbs. Torque manifold bolts in 15, 15, and 10 ft-lb increments until the final torque specification is reached.

Timing Chain and Gear Alignment

As illustrated in the photo above, line up the timing marks on the crank and cam sprockets.

Main Bearing Cap Torque Sequence

The main bearing caps need to be placed on the block in their respective positions on the registers and facing in the correct direction. You need to ensure that the main bearings fit correctly on the registers. Follow the correct torque sequence in this photo.

Distributor Firing Order

The firing order of the distributor is shown above, and cylinder position is designated above.

Engine Part/ Component	Stock Bolts/OEM Spec (ft-lbs)	ARP Bolts Using ARP Ultra Torque Lube (ft-lbs)
Main Bearing Caps	85	100
Connecting Rod Bolts	45	55
Head Bolts	70	80
A/C Compressor Engine Bolt	30	30
Balancer Bolt	135	135
Camshaft Locking Bolt	35	35
Carb to Intake Nut	7	7
Distributor Clamp	15	15
Exhaust Manifold Nut	30	30
Flywheel/Flexplate to Crank	55	55
Intake Manifold	40	40
Oil Pan	15	15
Oil Pump Cover	10	10
Oil Pump	35	35
Rear Main Seal Retainer	30	30
Rocker Shaft brackets	25	25
Starter Mounting Bolts	50	50
Timing Cover	15	15
Valley Pan End Bolt	9	9
Water Pump	30	30

ATI
6747 Whitestone Road
Gwynn Oak, MD 21207
877-298-5039
Fax: 410-298-3579
www.atiracing.com

CP Pistons
1902 McGaw Avenue
Irvine, CA 92614
949-567-9000
Fax: 949-567-9010
www.cppistons.com

Comp Cams
3406 Democrat Road
Memphis, TN 38118
800-999-0853
Fax: 901-366-1807
www.compcams.com

Competition Products
280 W. 35th Avenue
Oshkosh, WI 54902
920-233-2023
Fax: 920-233-1355
www.competitionproducts.com

Deano's Carburetors
1914 S. Buerkle Street
Stuttgart, AR 72160
870-830-5470rt, AR 72160
www.deanoscarbs.com

Edelbrock
2700 California Street
Torrance, CA 90503
310-781-2222
Fax: 310-320-1187
www.edelbrock.com

Hooker Headers
704 Highway 25 S.
Aberdeen, MS 39730 662 369-6153
(Tel)
www.hookerheaders.com

Jim Lewis Race Engines
217 E Lee Street
Vian, OK 74962
918-773-8075
www.jimlewisraceengines-cylinder
heads.com

MSD Ignition
1350 Pullman Drive, Dock #14
El Paso, TX 79936
915-857-5200
Fax: 915-857-3344
www.msdignition.com

Manley Performance
1960 Swarthmore Avenue
Lakewood, NJ 08701
732-905-3366
Fax: (732) 905-3010
www.manleyperformance.com

Meziere Enterprises
220 S. Hale Ave.
Escondido, CA, 92029
800-208-1755
www.meziere.com

Powermaster
1833 Downs Drive
West Chicago, IL 60185
630-957-4019
Fax: 630-876-2967
www.powermastermotorsports.com

RockerArms.com
19841 Hirsch Court
Anderson, CA 96007
530-378-1075
Fax: 530-378-1177
www.rockerarms.com

Smith Machine
472 N 2150 W
Cedar City, UT 84721
435-867-8106

Total Engine Service
9625 Humboldt Avenue S.
Minneapolis, MN 55431
952-888-3841

Total Seal
22642 N. 15th Avenue
Phoenix, AZ 85027
800-874-2753,
Fax: 623-587-7600
www.totalseal.com

Van Senus Auto Parts
6920 Kennedy Avenue
Hammond, IN 46323
219-844-2900
Fax: 219-989-7131
www.vansenusauto.com

CPSIA information can be obtained
at www.ICGtesting.com
Printed in the USA
LVOW05s0343141117
556116LV00026B/534/P

9 781613 252550